WRITING WITH *the* MOON

Writing with the Moon

Daily Practices to
Unlock Your Voice,
Write with Flow,
and Align with
the Power of Astrology

JACQUELINE FISCH

Copyright © 2026 Jacqueline Fisch

All rights reserved. No part of this publication may be reproduced, distributed, or transmitted in any form or by any means, including photocopying, recording, digital scanning, or other electronic or mechanical methods, without the prior written permission of the publisher, except in the case of brief quotations embodied in critical reviews and certain other noncommercial uses permitted by copyright law.

Published 2026
Paperback ISBN: 978-1-7365542-6-5
Ebook ISBN: 978-1-7365542-7-2
Library of Congress Control Number: 2026910050

Book design by Stacey Aaronson
www.thebookdoctorisin.com

Published by:
Sovereign Owl Publishing

For inquiries, please address:
hi@jacquelinefisch.com

Printed in the United States of America

Disclaimer: This book offers insights into food and wellness routines through the lens of astrology. It is not a substitute for professional medical care. The author is not a licensed nutritionist, dietitian, or physician. Readers are advised to consult a healthcare professional before making significant changes to their diet or lifestyle.

NO AI TRAINING: Without in any way limiting the author's and publisher's exclusive rights under copyright, any use of this publication to "train" generative artificial intelligence (AI) technologies to generate text is expressly prohibited. The author reserves all rights to license uses of this work for generative AI training and development of machine learning language models.

To the writers in my community who show up for themselves every day, make bold moves, and continue to achieve their business and writing goals.

CONTENTS

PART ONE

PART TWO

PART ONE

INTRODUCTION

"I'm a writer who's not writing."

I wasn't writing, and I felt shitty about it. I was writing a ton, but it was for my copywriting clients. I was also coaching a ton, helping clients write. None of this writing was for me.

It was the summer of 2019 when I gathered in a Zoom room with a handful of ladies in my mastermind group. Making this declaration felt like a confession.

On the surface, it looked like I had everything together. Growing a copywriting business and a new writing community, I took my job seriously. I dedicated all my working hours to writing for others. I met all my deadlines and put my client work first.

By now, I had been blogging for several years. Blogging was business, and I couldn't stop that. But what about *my* writing? The stuff that's just for me. The sentences that swirl in my mind in the middle of the night.

Almost two years earlier, I dedicated the whole month of November 2017 to writing my second book (the first was a fifty-page mini-book I muscled my way through in three months). I took part in a thirty-day writing challenge called National Novel Writing Month (NaNoWriMo), where the goal is to write 50,000 words in thirty days.

I did it, and then I didn't want to touch it. After letting it collect dust for a year, I picked it back up in November 2018 and completed a thorough round of edits. But the editing felt forced, like I was only rearranging words on a page, racing toward a finish line I couldn't see. Many of the words didn't mean anything. *What even was this thing? Certainly not a book I'd be proud to put my name on.*

The project gained a spark of new life after, unprompted, a clairvoyant told me my book wasn't self-development as I thought; it was a memoir.

I started making changes here and there in the manuscript to bring it to a place that felt whole and complete. But still, I was mostly ignoring my book, working on it sparingly.

What kind of coach am I if I can't finish my own book? I felt totally misaligned, like I shouldn't be giving anyone writing advice. Yes, I was putting *their* content first as a copywriter. But as an aspiring author, how could I call myself a writer if I was ignoring my own book?

The truth was, I was *thinking* about writing way more than I was actually writing. And it sucked. For months leading up to this point, getting any words out for my own projects felt painful, slow, and tedious.

I needed to stop all the forcing, so I decided to pull the plug on all of my writing—to stop thinking about it and simply accept that I wasn't going to write. I would keep the lights on in my business but no longer push myself to write when I wasn't feeling it. I also decided to press pause on blogging until the end of summer. My business would survive without that—or, so I'd hoped. I was also giving myself some grace because even though we moved states, got the kids situated in new schools, and I kept up with my business, I hadn't taken a breath.

That summer was a big lesson in surrendering.

By taking the pressure off, I was able to find flow in writing other things. Because crafting emails was always fun and easy for me—and they were less work than writing a blog—I turned my attention to email. And instead of continuing to feel shitty about my writing slump, I enjoyed focusing on emails, and in the work I did with my coach, I got clear on my personal and business values.

It turned out that to align with those values, my writing had to go back to the top of the list, and we agreed to commit three hours a week to my book project.

Three hours was a container, a guardrail—and it was a commitment I stuck to. On days when my book-writing time was cut short, I'd schedule it on my calendar and make it up later in the week.

Eventually, I finished the book and published it in April 2021, but for most of that project, the writing didn't feel good. I was frustrated with life, blaming everyone and everything around me for why the book still wasn't finished.

But really, it was all me.

Shortly before publishing that book, I discovered information about aligning my work and life with my menstrual cycle, which has four phases that correspond to the phases of the moon. At first, I simply paid attention to what was happening with my energy, and later, to the moon. After a few months of being in that awareness, I started syncing my writing, living, food, and movement with the moon cycle—and it clicked for me. Everything felt easier when I allowed myself to flow. Suddenly, it made sense why I didn't want to write that summer. I didn't need a psychic to tell me that I needed to write what my soul wanted to write.

What I realized is that I knew what to do, but I was missing the structure I needed to work with as I wrote.

Later that year, in alignment with the moon, I wrote my third book, *Intuitive Writing.* It felt like a huge weight had been lifted from my chest. The writing flowed and it was actually easy—so easy that I wondered if I was doing something wrong. Instead of ignoring my first draft for a year as I had the last time, I paused for only a few weeks and was excited to get back into it.

In short, I was flowing, not forcing.

And here's the kicker. It actually improved my business. Better clients showed up. Bigger projects landed in my lap. We started homeschooling the kids when they were entering the fifth and ninth grades. And the only thing I changed was my energy—which sounds like a small thing, but it's really everything.

By putting my writing first, I was sending strong messages to myself:

1. I'm important.
2. It's safe to be seen.
3. I show up and serve better when I put myself and my values first.
4. My work matters.

Now, writing is like breathing. My writing projects come first—always.

USING ASTROLOGY AS A WRITING TOOL

If you're wondering if you need knowledge of astrology to use this book, be assured that you don't. I'm not an astrologer. I'm a writer who uses astrology as a tool to help me write and live. More on this in a second.

In our natal chart, which is essentially a snapshot of the positions of all the planets at the moment of our birth, we each have our own astrology. In brief, there are twelve zodiac signs, and each one plays a designated role in a specific area of our lives. You can think of it as being made up of these twelve signs in certain ways. While we're not going to get into the details of individual astrology, this is just something for you to keep in mind.

Though we're not looking to astrology as a prescription for how to write, each zodiac sign provides possibilities for finding flow in your writing and editing. Flow in writing is when writing feels good—when you're calm, clear, grounded, well-balanced, and the words come out easily. This is what we're aiming for when we come to the page, as we bring our inner worlds forward and share our soul work with it. When we publish our writing, whether it's a memoir, business book, website, newsletter, blog, or social post, we're sharing a glimpse of our soul with the world.

Consider astrology as a tool to give us boundaries to contain our creativity. When we align with the day's energy (specifically, the moon, which we'll get to in a bit), it's like dressing for the weather. In the same way you want a sweater handy when it's cold and gray, or juicy watermelon slices when it's so hot your flip-flops melt on the sidewalk, we're considering the writing "weather." In other words, dressing for the weather is like writing with the weather.

Now, you may be asking:

Is it okay to use astrology if I believe in God?

And the answer is yes!

I believe in God, too—the Divine being that created the universe, the luminaries, planets, and living things. And no, there is nothing witchy or weird about writing using these remarkable creations within nature.

I, too, used to think writing with the moon was super strange. But being a Libra Sun, I'm practical *and* spiritual, so I easily see all sides of any story. So think of it this way: we all came from the Divine. I wrote this book while honoring my connection to God—and if you were drawn to this book, trust that divine nudge.

Probably the best way to think of it is that writing in flow is the doorway to expressing your authentic self. And tapping into your authentic voice is surrendering to divine guidance and allowing your innate nature, the universe, the moon, and/or your cycle to align your intentions with your actions and inaction.

If you're still feeling skeptical, and you derive inspiration or support from biblical passages, you may be heartened by the following references to celestial bodies in scripture:

> From the *Essene Gospel of Peace*:
>
> "And Jesus answered: 'Happy are you that you hunger for the truth, for I will satisfy you with the bread of wisdom. Happy are you that you knock, for I will open to you the door of life. For I tell you, that the Earth and the Heaven shall pass away, but my words shall not pass away, for my words are life and the Earth and the Heaven are born of me. For I am the Law, you are the branches, and my Father is the Sun, the Light, the Moon, the Stars, and the dew of the morning.'" Book 1, Chapter 1 (Note that here, Jesus connects his "Father" with the celestial bodies directly—blending nature and divinity.)

From the Gospel of Thomas:

"Jesus said, 'I am the light that is over all things. I am all: from me all came forth, and to me all attained. Split a piece of wood; I am there. Lift up the stone, and you will find me there.'" Saying 77 (This saying hints at a cosmic presence much like light, which in ancient times was thought to be connected to the sun, moon, and stars.)

From the New Testament:

"A great sign appeared in heaven: a woman clothed with the sun, with the moon under her feet and a crown of twelve stars on her head." Revelation 12:1 (Creativity often feels like carrying something bigger than you—a story, a message, a book that wants to be born through you. We're always doing so much more than putting words on paper; we're birthing something divine. The sun is clarity, vision, purpose, and the moon is intuition, cycles, mystery. Because you're breathing, you have everything you need to write.)

"After Jesus was born in Bethlehem in Judea, during the time of King Herod, Magi from the east came to Jerusalem and asked, 'Where is the one who has been born king of the Jews? We saw his star when it rose and have come to worship him.'" Matthew 2:1–2 (Your "star" is the writing idea that keeps nudging you. The Magi didn't know the whole path. Writers don't either—we follow the next hint of light.)

THE SUN (YANG) AND THE MOON (YIN)

Though we're focusing in this book on writing with the moon, we need to understand the sun, whose light the moon reflects.

* As a basic primer, the sun has a predictable twenty-four-hour cycle and is considered masculine/yang—carrying similar energetic qualities as men, who have a relatively consistent twenty-four-hour hormonal cycle.
* The moon is also predictable, but its cycle lasts about 29.5 days and is considered feminine/yin with four distinct energetic phases. These phases and energies have the same energetic quality as the four phases of a menstrual cycle and the four seasons (if you live where there are seasons; winter only lasts a week here in Florida!).

Masculine (sun/yang) and feminine (moon/yin) energy are woven into everything we do, and yes, that includes writing. Think of it this way: writing is surrendering and letting go (feminine) and also taking action (masculine). Editing is also about letting go (feminine) and taking action (masculine), doing the work to refine and carve out the details.

The masculine is the external leader, while the feminine is the internal leader. The feminine is the oracle, while the masculine warrior supports and carries her vision into reality. Feminine is being. Masculine is doing. They're both leaders in their unique ways, and they need each other. When working and existing with a balance of both, you can find groundedness, make magic, and truly experience the ebbs and flows we're supposed to experience, which also make for great writing and creative expression. Regardless of which energy is most dominant for us, we need both masculine and feminine.

Let's explore the notable qualities of each. As you explore this list, you might get some ideas about how to integrate the flavors into your writing practice.

Masculine/yang/sun	Feminine/yin/moon
Calm	Creating
Determined	Destroying
Focused	Embodying
Guiding	Engulfing
Holding space	Flowing
Logic	Free
Motivated	Giving life
Protecting	Intuiting
Providing safety	Leading
Rationality	Sensuality
Sensibility	Vulnerability
Strategy	Water
Strength	Way-showing
Supporting	Wild

Each astrological sign holds a predominantly masculine or feminine energy, alternating as we move through the zodiac, completely in balance with six masculine signs and six feminine signs. (As you read about each sign, you'll find a note about its masculine or feminine quality.)

The moon represents our inner world, emotions, soul, and

mood. When we work with the moon each day as writers, it's like adding lemon zest to your pasta, diffusing lavender essential oils in your office, or listening to classical music—in other words, influencing *how* we move through the world and let our words land on the page.

Here's how the moon phases line up with the seasons and a menstrual cycle:

- New moon / winter / menstrual phase
- Waxing moon / spring / follicular phase
- Full moon / summer / ovulation
- Waning moon / fall / luteal phase

Like us, the moon is constantly changing—it shifts zodiac signs roughly every two and a half days, and completes a cycle approximately every twenty-nine and a half days. As you start to pay attention to which sign the moon is in each day, you'll begin to experience how each day feels unique. How you feel at the beginning of the moon changing signs, as opposed to the middle and the end, can also be a little different as you get used to the energy.

A great writing coach shines a light on your blocks and hidden desires. With that in mind, I invite you to experience the signs that the sun and moon are in each day as your personal writing coaches. Like a coach, they never force you to do anything (they shouldn't, anyway). You always get to choose how you flow with the energy. Think of this book as receiving the daily advice of thirteen writing coaches—one for each sign of the zodiac, each with distinct personalities and moods—and me! Plus, you get a new one every couple of days. How could you ever get bored with your writing project with new energy and advice nudging you forward every day?

The key to writing with your unique flow is to write with the energy of what's going on, rather than fighting it or letting it fling you around. When you're present with what is, you can get intentional with your writing practice.

The truth is, you don't need a bunch of foundational information to write. You have everything you need already. I appreciate that people tend to want more efficiency sometimes and think things like, "I can't start this project until I do this other thing or until I read this book." You know that's not true. You can start with a little bit of information and awareness of what's coming up in your heart, and then write.

This book will support you in precisely that way.

Keeping in mind that your output should always be greater than your input—for a productive and feel-good writing life, anyway—I'll provide you with a small bite of information, and then you'll write. And we will keep the focus on writing intuitively—writing with your heart and soul (which has a direct line to God/Goddess/the Universe), over your brain and ego. Remember, it's flow, not force.

In anything you do, but definitely when you write, always tune into your body and intuition first. You might think the thoughts you have are your intuition speaking, but often they're just conditioning and other people's thoughts. Our true intuition—when we peel away the layers of who we think we are to who we truly are—is underneath all that. Don't discount the importance of your body. It's not only the vessel for your intuition, but the one doing the physical creating, writing, editing, and publishing.

While this book covers the moon specifically, and the moon phases roughly correspond to a season and phase of a menstrual cycle, use your discernment to apply the ideas that feel right to you and leave the rest. I like to work with the moon and then make small adjustments based on my cycle. If you don't menstruate or your cycle is unpredictable, simply work with the moon.

HOW TO USE THE MOON AS A GENTLE ARCHITECTURE TO FIND YOUR UNIQUE WRITING RHYTHM

When we pay attention to what's going on with our bodies and the planets, including the one we call home, it makes everything we're doing easier. It's like an extra boost of clarity, creativity, and focus—and we can choose what our project needs and use the giant battery we live on (the Earth) to fuel our inspiration.

Since 2020, I've been incorporating my cycle, the seasons, and astrology into my writing life. The results? I'm more peaceful every day, more confident, and more magnetic, productive, and creative than ever. I rest when it's time to rest instead of pushing to the brink of exhaustion. You're seeing the proof that it works—I flowed with the wisdom in these pages to bring this book to you. I also tested the materials here for several years with my writing community and private coaching clients.

The good news is that there are no hard-and-fast rules. You'll find detailed suggestions under each zodiac sign as you move into each of those sections, but the choices are always yours. If you notice any frustration with trying to fit the recommendations into a tidy box, realize that this could be fear talking, which tends to want to control things. Your soul doesn't need to control; it lets go and trusts. We want to write with our soul, because our soul trusts truth. Again, do what you feel is best for you, but be aware of what could be fear versus love driving you.

Let's explore the qualities of each moon phase and how you can align your writing with them to boost your likelihood of finding flow.

Moon Phase Overview

NEW MOON

When the moon is new, it's not visible from Earth because the sun and moon are aligned, with the moon between Earth and the sun. The side that faces Earth is in shadow. The new moon is like winter, a time to go within and plant seeds in the dark soil you'll later reap.

You might be more intuitive at this time. Because there's barely any light reflected back to us from the moon, we look inward for that light instead of from the noisy outside world. This can be an excellent time to make decisions. If I have a big decision to make, I'll ask myself during a new moon. I find I need time, rest, and space to reflect before I know what to do.

FIRST QUARTER (WAXING HALF MOON)

After the new moon, the light begins to grow. The right half of the moon (if you're in the northern hemisphere) is illuminated, and the left half is dark. This phase marks the halfway point between the new and full moon.

The waxing moon has spring-like energy, which has a buzzy, fresh, and juicy quality. Those seeds you planted in the dark are beginning to germinate and sprout, and they may start appearing now. You might begin a new writing project or open the doors for a new course or program you're running. Overall, you want to focus on things you want to grow right now, making it an ideal time for brainstorming brilliant ideas. What is swirling around in your mind? You'll naturally have more inspiration right now. Jot those ideas down. You may have some clever ones that surprise you.

If you feel overwhelmed by all these potential ideas and paths to explore, know that you don't need to take action on any of them yet. You've done your job by capturing them and will come back to one when the time is right.

FULL MOON

The moon is full when its entire face is fully illuminated and round, and it rises at sunset and sets at sunrise.

Consider this phase the climax, the culmination, the brilliant and clear spotlight and summer sun—when the plants are bursting with beauty and radiating in their full vibrancy.

You can also think of this as visibility time. Maybe this is when you'll share your work with the world, or plan your book release party or website launch. If you run an online business where you launch new programs and open your doors between the new moon and full moon, this can be a great time to close the door on your online sales because we're about to move to the waning moon, where the gesture is to let go and make space for something new.

In this phase, embrace that the extra light in the sky is a free jumbo spotlight shining on whatever you need to pay attention to, so you can let something go and express gratitude.

◗ LAST QUARTER (WANING HALF MOON)

After the full moon, it begins to wane. The left half of the moon (in the northern hemisphere) is illuminated, and the right half is dark. The waning moon has an energy like autumn. Pumpkin spice, fire-hued leaves, and harvest—all those seeds you planted in the dark are ready to be reaped. Think of a squirrel running around getting ready for winter—picking, gathering, and nesting.

As the light in the sky dims, we get ready to go back inside for winter again. Focusing, finalizing, completing, and buttoning all those things up—or letting them go if you don't want them to come with you into the next cycle.

CHOOSING WHAT TO WRITE

The advice in these pages will help you write whatever is on your heart—books, poems, website copy, emails, social posts, memes, a screenplay, and even an epic text message or love letter.

No matter what you choose to write, the advice here applies to everything. The members in my online writing community, which I've led since 2018, have worked on all the projects I just mentioned—and more. Since my clients mainly work on books and entrepreneurial writing, most of the suggestions you'll find here align with these kinds of projects.

You don't need to make your living as a writer to take advantage of the advice in the following pages. You might love writing (and I hope you do), or simply see writing as a powerful tool for communicating (it is), and use the suggestions here to help you bring your creative projects to life, get ahead in your career, share the words on your heart—or maybe all of these.

Whether you already love writing, or you discover or rediscover your fondness for the craft, you'll relish this cyclical writing adventure even more. In short: the more you enjoy writing, the more you'll *want* to write. So while it may feel challenging at first, like any skill, you'll improve as you dedicate yourself to practicing.

The thing about writing is that when you're *not* writing, you may either feel a buildup of inspiration or you may feel full of cobwebs. But once you begin writing, it's often like turning on a faucet, with more pressure built up than you thought. All sorts of ideas might come up, and you may wonder which one you should follow. Just know in this situation that there is no "wrong" thing to write. As long as you choose with your heart, you'll always pick the perfect topic. It's only when ego creeps in that we begin to second-guess our hearts or think we know better than Divine inspiration. Writing with the moon requires surrender and trust.

Now, if you have so many writing ideas that you don't know which one to choose, you're not alone. I hear this a lot from entrepreneurs and aspiring authors; first-time authors and new bloggers aren't the only ones with this perceived block. I also hear similar sentiments from second- and third-time authors, as well as people with tons of published work.

Writers usually share three and sometimes four or more ideas with me. If they're trying to choose a book idea, they look something like this:

> *"I have an online course, and I could easily turn it into a business book. It would be the 'smart' thing to do."*
>
> *"I've started writing about my personal experiences with [topic]."*

"There's this idea for fiction I want to write about that feels really exciting."

"I'm almost done with the draft of my book about [topic], so I could finish it and get it out there the fastest."

While these potential authors share their ideas so that I'll give them my expert opinion, what I do is feel their energy around each topic. I can usually immediately tell which book the writer should pick, but that's not my decision—it's one their soul already knows.

Sure, you could side with your brain on this choice and finish the almost-finished book—but are you excited about it?

You could focus on the book that will grow your business, but how much will your business actually grow when your heart is focused somewhere else and you're forcing yourself to make it happen?

You could write the book that feels like an easy win, then cross "write book" off your to-do list to be able to go on to write the next book, but how does that feel?

You may be surprised to learn that the writing I most feel is aligned with someone is not the book they describe with half a dozen "shoulds," or the one that seems smart, or the one that will skyrocket their business and make a boatload of money.

The book the writer should write is the one their soul wants to write.

I can practically hear you asking: "But how do I know what my soul wants to write?"

From my perspective, it's the one that, when you talk about it, your voice is a little shaky with enthusiasm—the one you keep circling back to yet won't focus on, the one that lights you up when you mention it.

If you're still unsure on your end, though, listen to your body.

Which ideas make you contract? Which ones make you feel expanded? This is the internal barometer you want to use. Pause to sense which feeling happens in your body, to listen to that inner voice.

And if you're still not sure?

1. Ask God to show you.
2. Write your list of book ideas. Notice if the one you really want to write jumps out at you.
3. Get quiet, close your eyes, feel your feet on the floor, and maybe the sun on your face.

   Take a few deep breaths. Breathe in the knowing that you can trust yourself. Exhale (maybe forcefully) all the chatter, others' opinions, and any limiting beliefs you have about any of the books.

   Spend a few minutes really feeling your energy.

   Now visualize. Let's say you see a book. See yourself writing your book, feeling completely in flow and totally free. Imagine holding your book out in front of you, sharing it with readers who have been waiting for you to write it. How does it feel? Where are you? What do you notice? What are you wearing? What do you hear, smell, and taste?

The book that wants to be written might have shown itself to you by now. When you see the book, you know for sure.

4. Open your eyes and look at your list. Does one jump out at you now? If it does, notice how your body is responding.

Does it feel exciting? Do you maybe feel a little nervous? Where in your body do you notice sensations?

5. If you're still unsure, try going down your list of book ideas one by one and ask your body to tell you yes or no. Your body only answers with yes and no responses. Anything more than this is your brain chiming in. We're asking your body because it's directly connected to God and can't lie. Read the list one by one and notice a yes or no, which will likely feel like expansion (yes) or contraction (no).

You might feel it in your gut and solar plexus area, or your heart. Simply pay attention.

If these activities still don't reveal your writing project, ask yourself two questions:

1. If money were no object, what would I write?
2. If status were no object, what would I write?

The overlap in your responses to these two questions will show you where your heart is right now.

Whatever your answer, trust it. It's important to teach your body that you trust it because the more you do, the clearer the signals it'll give you in the future.

Once you receive your answer, take action on it as quickly as possible—even if the only action you have time for in the moment is writing it on a sticky note with a few bullet points. And your other ideas? Trust that they are there for you when and if you're ready to revisit them. Keep them in a notebook or folder on your computer, knowing that when you're finished with your current project, you can come back to them.

What you want to do now is give your new writing project your main focus. You might have a full-time job, an overflowing client roster, a busy family, or all three. But yes! You can write your book no matter how busy you think you are. I've written books while working full-time for someone else, as a copywriter, and as a writing coach. I only started writing once I had kids, so it's all I know.

You might write for the first thirty minutes of each day, or spend a couple hours with your book on weekend mornings. However you choose to flow with the writing—BE the person with a published book. It's done, finished; your book is out in the world, changing lives. It even changed yours while writing it.

If it's another writing project you're working on—a finished website, dozens of blogs, a collection of poetry, then focus on BEing the person with these projects done, beautiful, and out in the world.

A LOVE NOTE ON EXCUSES

It's important to note that there's no judging or blaming—the moon, the weather, your cycle. Just as we don't point fingers at cold air for ruining our day, we prepare for the weather and put a sweater on. The moon doesn't control us. We simply get to use this energy as an opportunity, however we choose. We're not in control of external energy, but we can channel it to make the most of it and use it to work with ours, which we do control. Also, the other planets are always influencing us here on Earth. If you're interested, you can find an astrologer to help you decode what's going on in the cosmos for you personally.

In the first draft of this book, I intentionally put my blinders on so as not to let any astrologer's opinions guide the writing. When doing research, I had to look things up, but I was careful to discern others' personal views from my inner guidance.

What you're reading in this book isn't guidance directly from an astrologer. It's from a human tuned in, clearing my body and mind, and getting my information straight from the source. That source is God/Goddess, the Divine Creator we all have a direct connection to. You don't need this book to access it; you already have everything you need to write. This book provides a grounded framework. While I'm sharing my understanding with you in these pages, you get to create your own writing rhythm based on what information you receive that's right for *you*, based on your connection with God.

Some writers blame nature for why they can't write. "I'm just so full of inspiration during this waxing moon that I can't get to the page," or "It's the waning moon and I hate the world, so I can't edit my blog posts right now." The moon, the weather, and your body are never to blame. When you hear yourself say, "I can't do this," and follow it up with "because," I guarantee what comes next is an *excuse*.

You can be a great writer who makes no excuses. At the end of the day, it's you who's accountable.

HOW TO USE SUGGESTED ACTIONS AND WRITING PROMPTS

You'll find writing prompts for every zodiac sign and moon phase throughout this book—480 total. Writing prompts are great for getting you started if you need a boost. Think of prompts like a launching pad or caffeine for your writing. Use them to clarify, empty out, and witness what comes up so you can come to the page as a clear vessel. The clearer the vessel, the more impactful the writing.

While you might think you need to consume a bunch of information before you write—or finish this book—it's not necessary. Trust that you know enough already. You can start writing with only a sliver of information.

If you're following writing prompts, be aware of what's going on and what emotions are coming up, but don't believe everything you hear in your mind. Stay present to your emotions, but avoid letting them rule your day—and your writing projects. Journaling your way through what's coming up can help you spot the lies and places to heal—and then you can clear the lies and heal what needs healing. All so that you can write from a place of truth.

You might flow with your writing just fine without any prompts, too—it's all great.

If you do choose to work with suggested actions and writing prompts, choose as many as you like or do them all, keeping the following in mind:

1. Use the ones that apply to *your* writing project.
2. When you're journaling through a prompt, write fast, without thinking.
3. Follow the writing prompts using pen and paper to slow down your thinking brain and help you get into your body.

4. Because your body is where your intuition talks to you, simply tune in and listen.
5. Writing stream-of-conscious style on your prompts, jot down the first words that come to mind without judging, then launch into your writing for the day.

In each section, you'll find specific recommendations for your mind, body, and spirit. Try on the suggestions for one or all of these. You'll even find some plant-based, whole-food recommendations to help you fuel your writing sessions. Consider the foods that are local and in season for you as you choose what to nourish your body with—and, of course, what feels good to you.

Because how we do one thing is how we do everything, your writing output, or lack thereof, can be directly attributed to what you're putting in (or not) to your body and mind.

Speaking of your mind, you may want to turn off the news, stop scrolling through social media, and avoid reading about topics similar to yours in books and blogs. This is especially helpful when you're in a season of deep focus on a writing project. All that content will be available for you later when you're ready. And because writing will support your personal growth, chances are pretty high that when you've finished your writing project, you might not read the same things you're used to. Imagine all the time you'll save!

Remember: writing is a holistic and holy activity, and you are the vessel. You are energy, and your energy is infused into everything you write. This is why when we write with the natural rhythms around us—internally and externally—we're harnessing the power and transforming it into our creative work.

ADDING JOURNALING TO YOUR DAILY WRITING PRACTICE

The first time I heard the idea of working with the moon (and a menstrual cycle) several years ago, I decided to read about it and pay attention to what could positively influence my writing. At first, I didn't change anything about how I'd been working and writing; I started keeping notes and then jumped into exploring how I could apply it to writing over the course of a complete moon cycle. I invite you to do the same. Using a dedicated notebook, jot down these five things (for items 3 through 5, do an internet search or use an app, if you have one):

1. A few words about how you feel today
2. What season it is where you live (winter, spring, summer, fall)
3. What sun season we're in (one of the twelve zodiac signs)
4. What moon phase we're in (new, waxing, full, waning)
5. The moon sign of the day (one of the twelve zodiac signs)

Optional: What day of your cycle you're on (if you have one)

You might make these quick notes first thing in the morning, before bed, or both. It's a practice that'll take you no more than five minutes and will give you data to look back on to help you adjust your writing and life plans for the future.

FEEL-GOOD WRITING TIP: When journaling, you can write in any state. But if you're feeling anxious, nervous, or frustrated when writing something that someone else will read, pause and cultivate feelings of unconditional love, joy, and/or gratitude for yourself. By writing from a feel-good, positive state, you'll create more good vibes around your writing practice. Your readers will notice too.

HOW TO USE THIS BOOK

Because this is a book you can use right away, here's the no-messing-around approach to help you dive in immediately and do some writing with the unique energy of *today.*

STEP #1: GATHER THREE PIECES OF INFORMATION.

As with the journaling guidance, each day before you write, you'll peek at three pieces of information. Over time, you'll become familiar with these without needing to look them up.

1. Sun sign—where the sun is positioned in the zodiac today. The sun spends about a month in each sign.
2. Moon sign—what sign the moon is traveling through. Again, the moon travels through a different zodiac sign every two and a half days or so and goes through each sign in a 29.5-day moon cycle.
3. Moon phase—the current moon phase—new, waxing, full, or waning. The moon goes through four phases that last roughly a week. For simplicity's sake, loosely consider each of the four moon phases as approximately a week of calendar time. So, while the new moon, first-quarter moon, full moon, and last-

quarter moon each fall at an exact time, think about being immersed in the energy of that phase for roughly a calendar week. So if a new moon is on Monday, consider doing new moon things until Sunday, or until the first quarter moon. (Again, you can use an app or internet search for the current moon phase and sign. Be sure to make adjustments for your time zone. You can also check the Resources section at the end of this book.)

STEP #2: GET TO KNOW YOUR SUN, MOON, AND RISING SIGNS.

Known in astrology as the "big three," your sun, moon, and rising signs will help you know more about yourself, as well as your particular writing style and voice. Feel free to do this first or come back to this.

If you only know your sun sign, start there. (You can look up that section in the book for now, or you can visit astro-seek.com or astro.com to learn how to find your moon and rising signs, if you don't know them.)

You may want to revisit these three sections throughout the year to reflect and recenter yourself on who you truly are.

In each astrological sign section of this book, read the three categories that follow and notice what feels true for you. Stop reading when you get to the moon phase guidance (new moon, waxing moon, etc.). Right now, you're only looking for an overview of how you likely operate.

1. Your sun sign. Your sun sign is where the sun was on your birthday. It's your generator, inner spark, and driving force

that keeps you humming. This represents your ego and personality.

2. Your rising sign. Also known as the ascendant, this is the zodiac sign that was rising over the horizon when you were born. It describes how you present yourself physically to people you meet for the first time.
3. Your moon sign. We're pretty acquainted with the moon by now, so you know that the moon is your emotions, mood, and inner world. The moon receives and reflects sunlight. The people who know you best see your moon. Our inner world is how we write, so if you were to pay closer attention to any one of your big three, it would be this one.

There's also your chart ruler, progressed moon, the planets, and all kinds of fun stuff you can dig into if you're curious about astrology. We're keeping it breezy here, uncomplicating everything so you can do what you came here to do—write, edit, publish, repeat. You'll find your own cycle within nature.

For your daily writing, you'll follow three simple steps to gather some details about the writing mood of the day.

STEP #1: VISIT THE SIGN THE SUN IS IN.

Review the details of the sign and then stop before you read about the moon. We're focusing only on the sun at this step.

Think of the sun as a spotlight that influences the entire month. Once you read the sun sign section, you don't need to revisit it daily, unless you want a refresher. When the sun moves into the next zodiac sign, you'll then read that section. For example, if you pick up this book halfway through Taurus season, you'll read the Taurus section, stopping at the moon details, and then when the sun moves into Gemini (late May), you'll read that section.

STEP #2: VISIT THE SIGN THE MOON IS IN.

Remember the moon moves quickly, spending only about two and a half days in each sign. Read the intro section of the sign the moon is in, then visit the specific moon phase we're in and review the suggested actions and prompts for that phase.

Example: If it's Aquarius season (the sun is in Aquarius) and there's a full moon in Leo, you'll read the introductions for Aquarius and Leo, then review the full moon section in Leo.

Once you've read these instructions, this whole process should take no more than ten minutes. It'll take even less time once you're familiar with how to work with the materials here.

STEP #3: GO OVER THE CATEGORIES IN EACH ZODIAC SIGN'S SECTION.

SUN DATES — The sun visits each zodiac sign for about a month, so you'll have the dates handy. The date could vary by a day on either end based on where you live.

SYMBOL — Imagery is powerful. When we have a mental picture of the mood for the day, we know what to do. If I tell you the sun is shining and rainbows are peeking out after a day of cleansing rain, how do you feel? It paints a picture.

ELEMENT — There are four elements: air, fire, earth, and water. The elements correlate with nature's seasons.

MODE — There are three modes: cardinal, fixed, and mutable. These signify how the sign expresses itself and moves through the world.

- *Cardinal signs* initiate, lead, and pioneer. They're action-takers, ambitious, and easily start new writing projects—perhaps even setting trends.
- *Fixed signs* can hold onto things and follow through on an idea, or bring stability, determination, and persistence to the page. Harness this energy to bring reliability and focus, helping you build a sustainable practice and reach your writing goals.
- *Mutable signs* adapt quickly, bringing flexibility in how you write. They are good at going with the flow and for exploring many sides of an argument or situation.

ENERGY — Masculine or Feminine. This isn't about gender, but the predominant energetic quality of the sign.

RULING PLANET(S) — Each sign has a planet (or two) that shows us how we can move with the day, symbolizing its core energy, motivation, and natural expression.

HOUSE — One of the twelve sections of a birth chart that represents different areas of life, such as career, home, relationships, and money. Each house is associated with specific zodiac signs and planetary influences, helping to interpret how these energies can materialize in our lives. If you're new to astrology, no need to focus too much on the houses.

BODY PART(S) — Understand which parts of your body are ruled by the sign to give them some extra love, and simply become more mindful of these areas. You could do a little research and support these body parts with foods, herbs, spices, or teas.

PAIR — Also referred to as a polarity, but since duality and either/or thinking can be a trap, I prefer to see this as a pair. If finding flow feels challenging in a particular zodiac sign, we can look to the opposite sign to balance the energy. As an example, if the seriousness of Capricorn feels heavy and hard, look to the energy of the opposing sign of Cancer to bring some fluidity and emotion.

METALS — You may want to choose one to keep on your writing desk or wear as jewelry.

GEMS — These are to keep near you while you write. You might work some of these into your writing studio decor for the whole sun sign season, or simply hold one for the daily moon sign as you journal your way through some of the writing prompts.

COLORS — You can work the colors into your writing space with artwork, pens, candles, and notebooks—or even paint your toenails for the whole sun sign season. For the moon of the day's colors, dress for the "weather" by choosing an item of clothing or jewelry to enhance the mood of that day.

FLOWERS — You can weave these into your writing space, or even look at pictures of them before you begin writing.

ESSENTIAL OILS — Diffuse some in your space, or wear them diluted with a carrier oil, such as sunflower or jojoba, on your skin.

MANTRAS — Knowing the kinds of things each sign might say gives you a handy guide for how to move through your writing project for the day.

KEYWORDS — Use these actual words in your writing or editing, or simply embody the energy. A single keyword can spark tons of inspiration. Scan the list and write down any that jump out at you.

If you're reading these in the context of the sun sign season, you can use your favorites of these words as themes for the month. If you're looking at these in the context of the moon, use them for daily writing, or try some mash-ups by playing with the keywords of the sun sign season paired with the moon of the day.

CONTENT INSPIRATION — If you're not sure what to write about, consider writing on one of these topics. As with keywords, if you're reading these in the context of the sun sign season, you can write about these topics within the month. If you're looking at these in the context of the moon, use these for daily writing, or try some mash-ups by playing with the content of the sun sign season paired with the moon of the day.

WRITING WITH THIS SIGN — This section shows you the qualities of the sign and how you can best use the energy in your writing.

HIGH- AND LOW-VIBE EXPRESSIONS — This will show you how to embody the energy of the day's moon sign for feel-good writing. You'll also see some areas to keep a lookout for to keep your mood high-vibe.

NOURISHING BODY, MIND, AND SPIRIT — Because we're whole beings, we consider all three.

ACTIONS — Suggested actions follow for each moon phase, with four sets of actions in each sign.

WRITING PROMPTS — Discover ten prompts per moon phase.

INTUITIVE WRITING AND EDITING

Last, I want to revisit the topic of intuition, because it's crucial in all you're going to be doing in your writing projects.

The process I recommend for writing and editing is to use your intuition *first*. Your intuition speaks to you through your body, not your brain. I wrote the book on this process, it's called, ahem . . . *Intuitive Writing*. While I'd love it if you read that book too, you do not need to read it before you begin writing with the guidance in these pages. *Intuitive Writing* is a write-while-you-read book, so even if you think you want to read it first, there's no procrastination around here—only writing.

Here's all you need to know about intuitive writing and editing while working with the moon.

1. For the first half of the moon cycle, from the new moon until the full moon, the moon is waxing. Use this to write. Write what I call a Surrendered First Draft (SFD) — note this is not a Shitty First Draft as you may have known it. The next point explains the SFD.
2. While you're writing quickly, you're fully present, which means NO EDITING! Writing without editing as you go might be the biggest habit change you'll make with this process. It takes practice, but you can do it. Editing while writing slows us down. It taps into the thinking brain, which can lead to the *overthinking* brain. We know how far overthinking gets us (not very far at all), so I invite you to suspend the belief that you need to edit as you write. Writing fast without stopping is like writing as if you don't have a backspace button.

To help you write quickly, here are some strategies I love:

a. Write without looking at the screen so you can't see the red squiggly lines.

b. Look out the window or continually scroll up so you can't see the page.

c. Write in your native language and edit in the language you're publishing in.

d. Give yourself less time to write, which will prompt you to move faster.

e. Make the font super small or remove your glasses if you wear them, so you can't see what you wrote.

f. Write fast until around the full moon—or keep going until a few days after the full moon. The trick is to notice if you're full or empty. If you feel sufficiently emptied out every time you come to the page, you're doing it wonderfully. When you feel like you've written everything you can, switch to editing.

g. Let your drafts sit for at least a day or up to a month. If your book pours out in a couple of weeks, let it rest for at least a week before you dive back in. Let the words settle. When you go in to read, edit, and refine, the work will flow more smoothly.

h. During the waning moon—from the full moon to the new moon—read, refine, and edit what you wrote during the first two weeks of the moon cycle. Work in layers. As you read the guidance for each moon sign, you'll use the advice to help you edit with the mood of the day. Editing is never boring with fresh energy every couple of days!

To layer your edits, try a fast edit first, only fixing typos and the stuff your spelling and grammar checker flags. Then work in additional layers, a section at a time, adding emotions, sprinkling in personality, and tweaking whatever else your work needs. Intuitive editing is quick and doesn't second-guess—just like intuitive writing.

A FEW FINAL WORDS BEFORE YOU JUMP IN

I'm excited for you to begin this process, and hopeful you'll find it as fulfilling and grounding as I and all the creators I coach do!

Before you get started, some reminders to carry with you . . .

* We write with the moon's energy, while paying attention to the essence of the sun to get out of our heads and into our bodies.
* Our heads are still necessary—and there's a time and place for thinking with our left brains. But we don't want to be tapping into our brains for the entirety of our writing projects. It'll get too heady, and that's where we might find ourselves overthinking and overanalyzing, leading to the land of inaction—a land we drive directly past as writers.
* Big or small, action is the goal. Even if your action is five minutes of planning, that's enough.
* When you begin working with the rhythms of your body and the moon, it might feel a little foreign at first as you get

to know your body's signals and learn to trust them—especially if you're used to pushing through and following what you see everyone else around you writing.

* Or maybe you're on the opposite end and are ignoring your writing. It's taking up space in your brain just about every day, and you keep trying to "find the time" to write. I say this in quotes because you and I both know how "finding the time" goes.
* If this is your first time listening to your body and intentionally going with the flow, it might take some time to get there.

If you have a menstrual cycle, it might align with the moon phases, but no worries if it doesn't. You might find that over time, your cycle will naturally sync up with the moon as you pay attention to what's going on with your body and the moon. If you have a cycle and it doesn't sync up, see this as a bonus. You get two opportunities a month to experience the power of a full moon and ovulation—it's like double the power!

Finally, I designed this book so you can jump in no matter what time of year, season, or moon phase we're in. Many fresh starts suggest you wait to start until a Monday, the first day of a new month, or a new year, but not here. Around here, we GO. We take fast action and get our writing done.

Besides, chances are you've been stalling on your writing project for long enough already. This book is the antidote to blocks, overthinking, and procrastination. Even if you didn't plan on writing or editing today, guess what? You have everything you need to dive in.

And perhaps most important to remember: this is not about being perfectly aligned with every nuance of the moon. Even if you only do select activities, or are close to the cycles, the point is that your writing and your life becomes more *intentional*, and that connection to Nature and its rhythms is a beautiful thing no matter how you make it work for you.

PART TWO

ARIES

"Let's go!"

SUN DATES: March 21 - April 19

SYMBOL: The Ram — a ram rushes forward courageously and aggressively, taking life head-on and head down, and butts into its enemies. Historically, rams symbolized leadership. A ram's horn is also part of a cornucopia, the "horn of plenty," symbolizing abundance.

ELEMENT: Fire — the *spark*

MODE: Cardinal — initiating and moving forward

ENERGY: Masculine — courageously initiating without overthinking

RULING PLANET: Mars — the planet of energy, action, impulsiveness, courage, desire, and survival instinct

HOUSE: First

The first house is associated with self-image, the conception we project to others, first impressions, how we start things, physical characteristics, natural disposition, and self-interest.

BODY PARTS: head, brain, eyes, face, upper jaw and teeth, and adrenal glands. It rules the circulation of blood in the head.

PAIR: Libra

METAL: Iron — connected to power, courage, and protection

GEMS:

Diamond: focus, strength, and brilliance

Bloodstone: courage or endurance

Ruby: courage, athletic ability, and letting resentments go

Aquamarine: emotional equilibrium, courage, and strength

COLORS:

Red: assertiveness, courage, drive, raw energy, and passion

Scarlet: enthusiasm, intensity, and vitality

Mustard: energetic, optimistic, and slightly unconventional

FLOWERS:

Honeysuckle: change, courage, joy, wisdom

Tiger Lily: healing, protection, prosperity

ESSENTIAL OILS:

Cinnamon: warming, stimulating, and motivating

Ginger: invigorating and can boost confidence and courage

Peppermint: refreshing and energizing to boost focus and clarity

Bergamot: uplifting and can promote a sense of joy and enthusiasm

Clary Sage: clarity and insight, balances Aries's fiery energy

Frankincense: grounding and balancing

MANTRAS:

I am.

I'm just going for it!

I'm writing this "head-on."

KEYWORDS:

ability, active, aggressive, agility, assertive, beginning, bold, bravely, carve out, challenge, competition, courage, departure, discover, energetic, enthusiasm, expand, fast, fearless, fight, flash, fun, increase, increasingly, independent, initiate, intuition, lightning, more, motivation, number one, open, passion, pioneer, powerful, proactive, progress, public, spirit, start, suddenly, thinking, trailblazer, train, unique, vitality, winning

CONTENT INSPIRATION:

launching • going for it • visibility • standing up for your values • who you are • starting or finishing something big and being public about it • competition • edginess • blazing your own trail • initiating • self-image • first impressions • how we start new things • defense mechanisms • general outlook on life • sports • exercise • physical appearance

WRITING WITH THIS SIGN:

The first sign of the zodiac, Aries is a young sign with a beginner's mind—a beautiful mind for writing. It's spontaneous, reactive, and assertive. It challenges itself and knows that success is inevitable.

I started writing this book on the first day of Aries season to intentionally bring forth this initiating, big-book project, forging ahead without the overthinking kind of vibe to these pages. Sure, there were plenty of questions swirling in my head—*do I organize the book by sun sign or moon sign? Create separate sections for both? How do I bring in the essence of the moon phases to each stage as it relates to writing and editing?*

I quieted that mind chatter around 4:00 a.m. that morning and found myself grateful for choosing the first day of the Aries season to initiate my fourth book project—documenting a process that I've seen work so well for my students, clients, and myself.

Aries doesn't care about what you think. Aries says, "Screw it. Let's try it and see what happens." With Aries, we welcome a reprieve from overthinking and take action. We'll clean up the mess later. It's easier to stay out of your head with Aries—the head is busy ramming into things anyway.

Since Aries rules the first house, which is associated with how we start things, keep this in mind as you initiate your writing or editing for the day. *How* you write is just as important as what.

As a fire sign, know that fire isn't very reflective. Aries is an innovator, concerned more about the present and future than the past, so today might not be the day to dive into your emotional memories for memoir writing or storytelling. Save that for an earth or water sign.

Get going on your project with the fire and initiating energy. It can be especially helpful to move your body before writing. Trust your gut and start. Write the bold, hard thing—you'll have the confidence to push forward—and write in quick bursts. If Aries were to sign up for a running race, it wouldn't be a marathon—it would be a 5K. Fast and fun, see where you can bring that fun-run energy to your writing projects.

HIGH-VIBE ARIES: Takes charge and begins something new without a second thought or hint of doubt; writes in a self-assured manner; and brings a strong, clear, fiery energy to the page.

LOW-VIBE ARIES: Impatience and rushing to get going just for the sake of getting going. Try not to act like everything is an emergency or lose your cool because the writing isn't going your way or falling out of your fingers fast enough. Take a beat and step away for a minute to focus on something else, or take some deep, slow breaths (bringing in Libra's airy qualities, Aries's pair), then come back to your writing.

Nourishing Body, Mind, Spirit

BODY: Challenge your body today with a tough workout or add on some bursts of movement between exercises or at the end. Put your body first (this is good advice every day, but especially with a fire sign). Get up early, block time, and spend some extra time in the shower enjoying a scalp massage.

MIND: Skip the detailed plan and dive straight in. Figure out your plan later (if at all). Tune out all distractions so you can focus.

SPIRIT: Surrender to what's showing up, trusting that whatever is presenting itself to you is part of your soul path.

New Moon Actions & Prompts

New Moon Actions

- Make new moon intentions that are braver and bolder than anything you've envisioned before. Choose your words wisely, as you're always manifesting. Make your manifesting energy count and write them in present tense.

  Example intentions:

  I am so happy that my writing project unfolds quickly and powerfully.

  I'm so grateful to be someone who easily wakes up every morning at 5:00 a.m. to write for 30 minutes on my book.

  I am a powerful writer who consistently publishes blogs and social media posts.

- Begin with a brief outline and dive head-first into your project.
- Tackle the complicated writing you might have hesitated to approach until now.
- List all the actions you're taking—since there's not a lot of reflective energy going on, it might feel satisfying to do this.
- Explore where you can be more compassionate with your inner writer. Maybe something here will spark action on your writing project.

- Write out the details of your most fearless launch. Visualize how people feel signing up or reading, and how you'll celebrate.

New Moon Writing Prompts

I will start doing . . .

This will unfold quickly . . .

This lights my fire . . .

I've been undermining myself here . . .

When people read my words . . .

I take on this challenge with courage . . .

I could be more impulsive with . . .

I'm innovating . . .

I'm overcoming . . .

I'm the best ___ in the world.

Waxing Moon Actions & Prompts

Waxing Moon Actions

- Light a candle or three before writing today.
- Bring enthusiasm to the page as you take massive action.
- Invest a couple of focused hours at the page today with all your other browser tabs closed.

* Tap into the extra courage you have to take action and start your new writing project with a beginner's mind.
* Move your body before writing, especially if you're feeling antsy.
* Initiate, and write about the big, bold, hard thing you've been putting off.
* Review your plans and calendar for the next few weeks and see where they need some boldness and courage.
* Begin the writing that feels like risky business.
* Do some fast-batch writing. Set a timer for a few short bursts—10, 15, 25 minutes and write as fast as you can (no editing!) on a few different projects.
* Make your writing feel fun with a playlist that makes you feel alive and free.

Waxing Moon Writing Prompts

These are the actions I'm taking toward my writing projects . . .

I'm ready to be bold . . .

I'm excited about fun . . .

I'm here for . . .

I'm going for it . . .

I shine brightly . . .

Embracing every opportunity . . .

Carving out my own path . . .

Winning is . . .

This unfolds quickly and effortlessly . . .

Full Moon Actions & Prompts

Full Moon Actions

* Review the list of Aries keywords and write gratitude for how some of these things are showing up in your life. Write these as if they've happened.

  Examples based on Aries's new moon intentions:

  > *My writing project has unfolded quickly and powerfully. I'm so grateful—thank you!*
  >
  > *I'm so proud of myself for having the courage to start writing my book. Thank you for this powerful habit!*
  >
  > *I'm so grateful that I'm a powerful writer who consistently publishes blogs and social media posts. I love sharing my words with the world. Thank you, amen, and so it is.*

* Write several "I am . . ." statements as mantras using positive language.
* Take a fast walk and use your phone's talk-to-text feature to write a social post, blog, or book chapter to get the words out quickly. Then, put the transcript away and edit those words when the moon is waning (that's the next phase).

* Let yourself be as expressive as possible at the page today using colorful language.
* Walk in a different direction today or drive a new route with the intention of exploring and looking for new things.
* Refine the vibe you're giving off in your bio with some new words, and switch out your headshots with a new bold-feeling photo.
* Let go of impatience, anger, frustration, jealousy, worries, and impulsiveness.

Full Moon Writing Prompts

I'm fearless . . .

My energy is best . . .

I'm going for it . . .

I focus . . .

I'm expressing . . .

I'm grateful to have overcome . . .

I'm number one . . .

I challenge myself . . .

I walk my own carved-out path . . .

As a trailblazer . . .

Waning Moon Actions & Prompts

Waning Moon Actions

* Simplify your writing through a round of edits focused on what you really want to say.
* As you review and edit today, ask yourself, "Is this clear enough?" and "Could a fifth-grader understand this?" Simplifying your writing is an act of service for your readers.
* If you notice you censored yourself as you wrote your draft, add the bold thing you might not have had the courage to say before.
* Say what you want to say. Have faith that the right message will come out when you take a deep breath and trust.
* Dive into an editing challenge—the ram can go head-first into the challenge and push its way through.
* If your first draft was a little swear-y, do a search of your document to see how many curse words appear. In sales copy, swearing can result in fewer conversions; too much in books and blogs can be distracting. But a well-timed f-bomb can go a long way, so swear mindfully.
* Take advantage of your keen eye for detail and relentless focus.

Waning Moon Writing Prompts

I'm no longer censoring . . .

The only opinion about this that matters is mine . . .

No more overthinking . . .

I'm focused and will finish . . .

I'm determined and I'm totally ignoring . . .

My authenticity . . .

Pioneering . . .

Suddenly . . .

I'm grateful these troubles are gone . . .

I enjoy the challenge . . .

TAURUS

"I persevere!"

SUN DATES: April 20 - May 20

SYMBOL: The Bull — a symbol of strength, tenacity, virility, and power. Left alone, a bull will happily graze (ahem . . . write), but if he's bothered, he'll charge! Taurus is known for its calm and peaceful demeanor, but when angered, watch out.

ELEMENT: Earth — the foundation, like grass or a meadow

MODE: Fixed — move steadily and consistently

ENERGY: Feminine (even if its symbol the bull is a dude) — grounding ideas and developing patiently

RULING PLANET: Venus — symbolizing love, money, pleasure, grace, beauty, and art

HOUSE: Second

The Second House represents your values, resources, and sense of security, including how you earn and spend money. It's about material and personal stability and growing what you truly value.

BODY PARTS: throat, neck, ears, jaw, lower teeth, thyroid gland

PAIR: Scorpio

METAL: Copper — beauty, love, artistry, and sensuality

GEMS:

Emerald: associated with Venus in preserving love

Rose Quartz: self-love, protection

Diamond: strength, commitment, endurance

COLORS:

Green: abundance, growth, stability

Yellow: warmth, optimism, clarity

Orange: creativity, vitality, comfort

Brown: grounding, reliability, security

Soft Pink: nurturing, calm, affection

FLOWERS:

Rose: love, beauty, passion

Poppy: rest and imagination

ESSENTIAL OILS:

Rose: calming and uplifting, love, emotional balance, aligns with Taurus's appreciation for beauty

Patchouli: grounding, stability, and a connection to nature

Sandalwood: relaxation and promoting comfort

Lavender: calming, peaceful, serene

Bergamot: mood booster and joy

Ylang Ylang: love and sensuality

MANTRAS:

I have.

I am beautiful.

I am love.

KEYWORDS:

abundance, accumulate, aesthetic, art, asset, blessed, calm, certain, comfort, completion, consistent, continue, convenience, craftsmanship, earnings, earthly, expertise, faith, finances, finishing, flourishing, generous, grounded, high-class, income, innate, lavish, lifestyle, luxurious, money, natural, organic, patience, peace, possessions, prosperity, real, reliable, security, sensibility, serenity, simple, steadily, steady, stability, sustain, texture, valuable, wealth

CONTENT INSPIRATION:

follow-through • completion • serving customers as opposed to trying to find new ones • staying grounded in who you really are • tuning into yourself • green, earth, plants, flowers, trees • texture • grounding • your body of work • your legacy • defining your values • healthy routines • being in nature • ecology • generosity • sense of self-worth • personal possessions • speech/the throat • our ability to provide for ourselves

WRITING WITH THIS SIGN:

Aries initiates and gets us moving, and Taurus keeps going to create abundance and wealth.

Persevere slowly and mindfully through your writing project today. Tap into the strong, stable, "bull-headed" energy to lock onto your goal and be relentless about making progress—tremendous or tiny. You can use this persistent fixed energy to work for you and support your writing goals.

How Taurus writes could be just as important as what Taurus writes about. Sit in your reliable spot where you know it's practical for writing to happen. Look to your writing space to provide comfort and security, like a favorite cozy blanket, candle scent, or essential oil—maybe even working in one of the scents mentioned for Taurus.

Now, notice how sensual your writing space is. Does it feel nurturing and serene? Does it feel good to you? You may want to examine all the other areas of your life, too, to make sure everything is in good grounding order.

Earthy vibes will feel nurturing and grounding. Maybe you'll write outside, at a cafe on a patio, while moving just a little slower, taking your time to communicate, all while looking after yourself.

Slow down and savor the writing process. How can you tune into your body and feel what it's trying to say right now? Maybe there's a luxurious and passionate quality in your writing that wants to come through.

HIGH-VIBE TAURUS: Your readers rely on you to show up with a new piece of writing when you said you would. Come to rely on yourself and trust your hard work is paying off. Let every aspect of your writing practice be satisfying—from your food to movement to drafting and editing—and draw deep pleasure and connection from the entire writing process.

LOW-VIBE TAURUS: Getting annoyed about interruptions. Author Julia Cameron saw interruptions as corrections in trajectory. If you're in your focused writing flow today and it comes to an abrupt halt, take a deep breath before reacting. Being lazy about your writing practice, taking shortcuts, not wanting to do the work, and inflexibility are also low-vibe expressions if they become toxic. It can be an effort to get that big bull moving. Taurus might also write tons and publish very little, keeping everything to itself and allowing it to stagnate. See where you can tap into the opposite sign of Scorpio for its intensity to help you get going.

Nourishing Body, Mind, Spirit

BODY: Ground today before writing and throughout the day as often as you can by putting your bare feet on the earth (if it's safe—use your judgment). Make sure you're physically comfortable, including in the clothes you choose to wear, and sip something warm throughout the day. A slow, sensual yoga practice with essential oils diffusing nearby may help you feel calm and in the flow. If you're feeling amped up, moving some extra heavy weights around might also feel good, and you'll feel powerful AF—*strong like bull!*

MIND: Slow your mind down. Use it to sink into your body and notice how you feel. Commit to a routine to support your body without having to think too much.

SPIRIT: What does your soul want to say? What would feel good to express? Maybe it's something that's been kept quiet for too long.

New Moon Actions & Prompts

New Moon Actions

- Put your bare feet on the ground and ask, "Who am I?"
- Eat nurturing food from the earth—maybe healthy versions of your childhood favorites.
- Create a designated writing spot that feels luxurious.
- If you're writing about a new-to-you topic and it's not flowing, be patient with yourself and the process. Trust that flow will come—it just needs to find you working. Even if it's fifteen minutes, settle in at the page and start moving your fingers.
- More than just setting new moon intentions, create a practical plan of action steps so you know what to do next and keep from stagnating.
- Focus on the practical details of your writing plan.
- Explore your relationship with writing and money.

New Moon Writing Prompts

My writing routines and habits need some grounding here . . .

I can serve my current customers even more powerfully . . .

I love . . .

I'm grounded in . . .

This is deeply nurturing . . .

Thank you . . .

Yes, more, please . . .

I create abundant flow with my words . . .

I anchor . . .

I have clarity now . . .

Waxing Moon Actions & Prompts

Waxing Moon Actions

* Take your time to write your drafts today. Go slow and savor the experience. Pay attention to your throat as you write and breathe.
* As you write, make sure you're writing how you'd naturally speak. Read it aloud to check for any words you wouldn't naturally say.
* If the words aren't budging onto the page, grab your phone and try some talk-to-text while taking a walk or sitting in nature. Taurus rules the throat, so speaking may be easier than writing today, though writing is still an expression of your voice.
* Build a predictable routine to help you anchor your writing habits. Maybe you'll create designated spots in your home for certain kinds of writing, such as writing drafts on your couch and editing at your desk.

- Changes and new topics could feel jarring today—see how you can accept this and know that if you pause and stay open, you might become more comfortable with the shift later as the moon changes signs.

Waxing Moon Writing Prompts

When I make progress on ___, I feel ___.

This might be complicated now, but I trust this is simple under the surface.

I'm bringing relentless focus to . . .

I value . . .

My writing routine . . .

I'm pushing toward . . .

The last time I saw something through . . .

I sustain . . .

I will complete . . .

I succeed in writing . . .

Full Moon Actions & Prompts

Full Moon Actions

- Since the full moon energy sticks around for about a week, set up your writing life for the next several days—your space, food, movement, schedule.

* Focus and follow through, while staying open to where you might need to change course.
* Write the hard thing directly from your heart—the thing you can put your head down (and bull horns up) and stay committed to seeing through.
* While you might normally want to avoid messy writing so you can follow the tried and true predictable path, use your focus and determination to bring practicality to the mess and order to the chaos.
* Take your time communicating and being mindful of the power of your words.
* Remember: pleasure. Maybe even write it on a sticky note, and keep it where you'll see it as you work to recenter yourself back to pleasure if you find yourself stressed or feel some tension in your neck.
* Notice any areas of your writing life, or in pieces of writing, where you're stubbornly holding onto anything.
* Let go of anything keeping you from expressing your voice authentically.

Full Moon Writing Prompts

While writing, I noticed . . .

I need . . .

I find pleasure . . .

I'm going to say this even if I'm scared . . .

Slow and steady . . .

I let go of any ideas of scarcity . . .

There are always infinitely more things I can write about . . .

I'm certain . . .

I see increasing . . .

I relish the writing process . . .

Waning Moon Actions & Prompts

Waning Moon Actions

* Revisit your body of work and write gratitude for your favorite creations.
* Review your list of unfinished projects. Choose one project and a target completion date. What resources do you need to finish it? Who can help? Write it on your calendar and plan your finishing strategy.
* Do a practicality edit to your writing today, simplifying unnecessarily complex words, shortening sentences, and removing repetition.
* Read your writing aloud as you revise, and ask yourself if it's clear and easy to follow.
* If you're feeling stubbornness kick in and not wanting to change your writing, notice where you can soften and be open to change that will serve and nurture yourself (and even your reader).

Waning Moon Writing Prompts

I'm so glad I wrote . . .

I'll finish ___ before ___ and it will feel ___.

To finish my writing project, I need . . .

I'd rather be at peace about . . .

I'm softening . . .

I bring stability to . . .

This brings safety . . .

I'm fulfilled . . .

With this, I have more than enough . . .

This habit brings comfort . . .

GEMINI

"I wonder what will happen."

SUN DATES: May 21 - June 20

SYMBOL: The Twins — represent the dual nature of Gemini. They also symbolize relations, exchange, and interaction. Super adaptable and flexible, sometimes to the point of presenting as two different personalities. The dualistic nature of the sign also embodies the union of intellect and intuition.

ELEMENT: Air — the movement of air like a breeze moving through leaves, collecting ideas and connecting information

MODE: Mutable — adaptability and flexibility

ENERGY: Masculine — outward, conversational, sharing thoughts

RULING PLANET: Mercury — the planet of day-to-day expression and communication. Mercury's action is to take things apart and put them back together again.

HOUSE: Third

The Third House represents communication, thinking, and the kind of learning we do daily. It also relates to writing, speaking, curiosity, and the exchange of ideas and thoughts with your close environment (think: siblings, neighbors, and the local community).

BODY PARTS: shoulders, arms, wrists, hands, fingers, upper lungs

PAIR: Sagittarius

METAL: Quicksilver — the old name for the metal mercury, representing rapid or unpredictable movement or change

GEMS:

Agate: strength and its ability to reduce stress, dizziness, and headaches, making it particularly useful for calming mental overstimulation

Emerald: clarity, communication, curiosity, love, mental harmony, and intellect

COLORS:

Blue: communication, clarity, expression

Yellow: brilliance, curiosity, playfulness

Green: adaptability, change, growth, learning

FLOWERS:

Lily of the Valley: love, happiness, humility

Lavender: refinement and elegance

ESSENTIAL OILS:

Peppermint: invigorating, stimulating focus

Lemon: uplifting, clarity, positivity, curiosity-enhancing

Lemongrass: mentally rejuvenating, boosts memory

Bergamot: balances the dual nature of Gemini, promoting emotional stability while encouraging communication

Rosemary: mental clarity and memory enhancement

Lavender: calming to balance restless energy

Eucalyptus: clears the mind and promotes a sense of openness

MANTRAS:

I think.

I express.

I am strong.

KEYWORDS:

adaptable, blogging, both, changeable, collaboration, coming together, communication, connection, conversation, cool, curiosity, easily, either, eloquent, fascinating, flexible, fresh, friendly, humor, information, inquisitive, intelligent, joke, knowledge, light, mental, multiple, mutable, negotiation, neighbor, newsletters, responsive, rhythmically, simultaneously, sociable, social media, study, superficial, talkative, versatile, vibrant, wild streak, wisdom, wit, words, work, writing

CONTENT INSPIRATION:

communication styles • relationship dynamics • create ideas around duality and where you arrive on opposite ends of the spectrum • co-creation • challenging communication • collaborations • socializing • networking • play • fun • trips • commuting • transfers • travel • childhood • partnerships • grasping an idea • teaching something new • social media tips • lived experiences

WRITING WITH THIS SIGN:

"*I'm so inspired!*" All the words, ideas, and inspiration are coming through. Multitasking might even feel good with a Gemini moon.

Of course, do so mindfully to maintain the quality and integrity of your work. In this energy it can be natural to be all up in your head. Remember you have a body, too—honor it appropriately.

Make sure you're giving yourself time at the page that feels fun and joyful—whether that's inside the comforting pages of a notebook or on your computer. Otherwise, the words might feel like they're stuck or blowing around within the walls of your busy mind with no outlet. Let them out so they can be free!

See every chance you write as an opportunity. There's not a lot of emotion with a Gemini moon, which is great for writing things that may have felt too emotional or challenging to tackle in the past—certainly when the moon was in a water sign. Use this as an opportunity to easily put emotions aside and take action on the writing you know you need to get out there. Tackling the tricky piece can feel rewarding right now. Go for it!

This is also a fun time to explore new writing tools, formats, and platforms; break out of (and throw away) the box; or build a better box (or maybe an airplane!). It's an opportunity to allow the fullness of creative expression, connect with your community, and take action to make the world a better place.

Connect with your most optimistic, cheerful, friendly, fresh, and lighthearted self in your words. Use this time as a welcome invitation to take your words less seriously and invite some play into your writing style, practice, and habits.

HIGH-VIBE GEMINI: Embracing variety in your writing types, content sharing, and day-to-day activities. Intentional task switching and oscillating from one idea to the next might feel energizing.

LOW-VIBE GEMINI: Notice where your writing is sacrificing clarity in place of cleverness, or where you may be falling into worry or grumpiness. You may agonize over how your message will be received and wonder what others will think of your writing. Tap into fiery Sagittarius to take bold, wise action and give the wind something to fan with the flames of Sag.

Nourishing Body, Mind, Spirit

BODY: Change up your writing scenery. Take a short writing excursion to somewhere you normally wouldn't write—even if it's within your own home. Pay attention to your breath as you write today. Practice slow breathing as you type. If you catch yourself holding your breath as you write, pause, take a deep inhalation with a longer exhale, and return to your writing.

MIND: Stimulate your mind by writing about a new-to-you topic, or listen to a new-to-you playlist while you write and edit today to change up the energy. Research something that's been coming up for you in conversation lately.

SPIRIT: Listen to the words between the words and read between the lines in every exchange you read or hear today.

New Moon Actions & Prompts

New Moon Actions

* Notice the exact words people use—both spoken and written.
* Listen closely to your readers, clients, and the language you hear and see as you go throughout your day. Simply become aware of the language people use. You might jot down some of the words and phrases that pique your curiosity. You might not know why a particular word or phrase sticks out to you, but write it down anyway; it could be your intuition nudging you.
* Make a plan this moon cycle to learn something you've always wanted to learn.
* Think about potential collaborations or co-creators to help bring your projects to life.
* Do some analysis, sort data, group, and organize your writing projects.
* Create some outlines (if you like that sort of thing).
* Make some plans to help you make sense of where you're going in your writing project.
* Plan a workshop to teach in the next few weeks, or attend one.
* Plant some seeds and start scheduling calls around the waxing and full moon to have conversations with others

and expand your thinking. Trust that with every meeting you have, you invite chances for your intuition to speak.

New Moon Writing Prompts

I wonder . . .

I'm here to express . . .

I radiate . . .

I'd like to improve my communication by . . .

My favorite co-creation . . .

I co-create . . .

This is stimulating and exciting . . .

I'm curious . . .

I intend to ride the wave of opportunity . . .

I attract the best . . .

Waxing Moon Actions & Prompts

Waxing Moon Actions

* Play some upbeat music, set a timer for fifteen minutes, and dive into a delightful brainstorming session. When you're generating ideas, let all those seemingly scattered options flow onto the page without judgment or question. Let them out. Just because you write something down as an idea, it isn't a commitment to write about it. Brainstorm quickly and let it sit.

* Batch some drafts of your content—blog drafts for the coming months, images or video clips with captions for the week, or even a newsletter to spark connections.
* Write fast drafts on a few different topics, or jump around in your book, writing different chapters.
* Get curious about the words you use in your website copy and the language that often comes through in your content and book writing. Explore some definitions to see if the word has the right connotation for you. Are there words that are more aligned or feel better to use? A thesaurus is your best friend right now!
* To find more words to express your message, do a web search for images of your content and see what comes through.
* Enjoy the chattiness of the day and comment on social media. Ask questions on social media and with anyone you spend time with in person.

Waxing Moon Writing Prompts

This is wrong for me . . .

This is right for me . . .

This idea might be for someone else . . .

I want to know this about my reader or audience . . .

This is the opposite of what I believe . . .

I need to have this difficult conversation . . .

I imagine . . .

I take action enthusiastically . . .

Expanding my horizons . . .

I use beautiful words that feel good to write . . .

Full Moon Actions & Prompts

Full Moon Actions

* Reach out to potential collaborators, join a local networking group, and wear a vibrant shade of blue, green, or yellow if you attend a networking or social meeting today. Socialize, network, play, and have fun.
* Send some friendly emails to people in your network.
* Get social in the comments on blogs and social media and leave thoughtful notes or perspectives.
* Look at your writing project and think about where you can make it better. What quick improvements could you make to your website copy, sales pages, social bios, or author bio?
* Review your writing bucket list—or create one if you haven't—and only include expansive ideas.

Full Moon Writing Prompts

I collaborate . . .

When I partner with ___, this is the kind of magic that happens . . .

I'm smiling at . . .

My love language is . . .

If I were to receive two things at once, they'd be . . .

My favorite thing about social media is . . .

The message I'm here to spread . . .

I'm getting perspective on . . .

I trust that I know what to write at the perfect time . . .

I balance my writing with joy . . .

Waning Moon Actions & Prompts

Waning Moon Actions

* Empty that full mind into your journal before writing anything else.
* Channel that busy bee brain into making a lot of progress or completing a project.
* Add some dialogue to your memoir.
* Craft some first-person statements for sales copy, a blog post, or a social post.
* Review your consultation notes from conversations with potential clients and see if you're using their exact words. This is an exercise in active listening.
* Schedule some quiet time to take a break—napping, meditating, walking mindfully—whatever you need to stay present and slow the busy energy.

- Do an edit to weave in a conversational tone. Read your writing to see how you'd naturally speak. Using contractions is an easy way to make your writing feel conversational.
- If you're editing a piece of writing you've spent a lot of time reviewing already, read it from the bottom to the top, one sentence at a time. Our minds might be better at attention to detail now, so use this energy to catch those little typos.
- Do a clarity edit on your writing—use a clear word in favor of a complex one.

Waning Moon Writing Prompts

My work solves this problem . . .

My favorite client is . . .

My ideal reader . . .

I complete . . .

I ground my inspiration into . . .

I speak . . .

I'm letting go of overwhelm here . . .

I can teach others . . .

I let go of a lack of focus . . .

Writing is stimulating . . .

CANCER

"I'm open."

SUN DATES: June 21 - July 22

SYMBOL: The Crab — a crab can walk and run sideways, so Cancer can move with the flow of their lives and throughout their words in a scurrying manner. Consider a crab's hard shell—it's designed for self-preservation, but under that solid cover, it can be sensitive and retreat inward when wounded.

ELEMENT: Water — fast-moving from a local source, like a creek or river

MODE: Cardinal — writing and editing directly or with emotional intensity

ENERGY: Feminine — creating connection and emotional safety

RULING PLANET: The Moon — representing our most profound personal needs, primary habits, reactions, emotions, and unconscious. Where the sun acts, the moon reacts. The moon is both our inner child and our inner mother. It's responsive, receptive, and reflective. The moon represents our spontaneous and automatic reactions and serves as a mediator between our inner and outer worlds.

HOUSE: Fourth

The Fourth House symbolizes the home, roots, and emotional foundations. It reflects your inner world and where you feel safe and nurtured.

BODY PARTS: stomach, breasts, womb, lower lungs, uterus, bladder

PAIR: Capricorn

METAL: Silver — wisdom, beauty, age, and grace

GEMS:

Pearl: integrity, loyalty, wisdom, and calm

Opal: originality and confident creativity, allowing you to express your true self

Emerald: promoting healing, balance, and harmony

Moonstone: deepening intuition, helping with transitions, and nurturing nature's rhythms

Cat's Eye: confidence, balance, grounding, and uplifting

COLORS:

Silver: intuition, reflection, emotional sensitivity

Violet: spirituality, healing, imagination

White: purity, calm, emotional clarity

FLOWERS:

Water Lily: the spiritual process of moving toward enlightenment

Magnolia: endurance, perseverance, longevity

ESSENTIAL OILS:

Frankincense: emotional support, spiritual growth, calming, intuition

Tulsi/Holy Basil: emotional balance, reduce stress, and enhance intuitive abilities

Myrrh: emotional stability and healing

Lavender: calming, soothing

Blue Tansy: calming

MANTRAS:

I feel.

I nurture.

I reflect.

KEYWORDS:

appreciate, approachable, belonging, caring, childhood, comfort, connection, conservative, contemplative, deep roots, defensive, emotions, family, feelings, fierce, friendly, fulfilling, gentle, going deeper, help, home, kind, kindred spirits, loving, meal, mother, nourish, nurture, parenting, power, protect, recharge, relatable, relocate, renovation, replace, safety, self-compassion, self-love, self-trust, soothe, support, sympathize, warm

CONTENT INSPIRATION:

nurturing leads • creating or revisiting any email sequences with the mindset of "loving the one you're with" • nurturing your customers and readers more deeply • listening to your customers • going deeper with your clients • reconnecting with your audience • nourishing yourself, your clients, your audience, and your readers • adding an emotional layer to your writing while editing quickly •

belonging to a family or community • renovating • relocating • replacing habits • creature comforts • where you can be approachable and relatable in your writing

WRITING WITH THIS SIGN:

Since crabs tend to shield themselves from hostile environments, they're not the first ones rushing into change. It's simply too uncomfortable and can bring up feelings of being unsafe. However, if the crab scans the environment first, it can settle—just like you can settle in to write when it's clearly secure enough to do so.

As the crab might conceal itself in the wild by decorating its body with plants and animals, that tendency could show up as hiding in your writing too—hiding behind a brand name, pen name, or avatar. Crabs aren't the ones making the big splashes—they'd rather blend in or move quickly along.

Cancer is the most emotional sign, and the moon loves traveling through these "feely" waters. Water signs have a reputation for being emotional and flowy, but as you're writing, pay attention to water's other strong signature—power. Water can create or destroy. Water needs boundaries to feel safe. And Cancer is fast-moving—picture a fast river, which is quite different from deep, still, intense Scorpio water and the multi-faceted Pisces water that sprays all over the place.

Cancer rules the home—but know that you can create the essence of feeling at home wherever you are with familiar objects. Writing at home or in a nurturing space could be nonnegotiable today. If you're away from home, you can wear your comfortable clothes, sip a familiar tea, and enjoy comfort foods.

You may find some opportunities to savor the sweet, nurturing depth of some emotional writing. Go slow today and wade into the water—now's not the time to jump into the deep end with both feet. The water is moving quickly, and unless you're ready to be taken downstream, pack a floatation device. Reminisce about childhood things with kindness and gentleness. This could be a good time to write those memoir essays that explore the events of your childhood.

HIGH-VIBE CANCER: Honoring your authentic writing voice and saying a hard no to anything superficial. Trusting your intuition and intuiting your readers' and clients' needs. Writing quickly and forcefully—like a strong current.

LOW-VIBE CANCER: Accumulating piles of words and keeping them hidden from the world under a hard exterior. The piles of unpublished words can lead to a feeling of inner safety. Watch out for loose boundaries around emotions and protect your sacred writing time. Absorbing negativity and getting lost in it could lead to complaining. You might get stuck in your emotions and notice an inability to call on the brain to find balance. Indecisiveness around which writing project to start, focus on, or finish could come up—find your calm in the raging waters and trust your inner guidance.

Nourishing Body, Mind, Spirit

BODY: Eat delicious food, perhaps healthier versions of childhood favorites, especially of the unprocessed variety. Aim to create a comfortable environment before, during, and after writing. Look around before you begin writing to create a sense of safety for your nervous system.

MIND: Instead of believing every emotion and letting it rule your day or trigger you, stand back and look at the whole picture. Try to see the whole river flowing, not just a choppy sliver.

SPIRIT: Burnout is impossible if you're in the flow and writing about things aligned with your higher self.

New Moon Actions & Prompts

New Moon Actions

- Move quickly and surrender to the words that want to come through as you write.
- It's a good time for healing your inner child and any limiting stories you're telling yourself around writing.
- Process your emotions through journaling.
- Visualize how you'd like to be nurtured, continuing to nurture your inner writer.

* Brainstorm some personal tidbits or aspects from your home life that you can comfortably weave into your website's about page or bios.
* Write in places or about things that positively remind you of the past.
* Plant seeds for a happy writing life filled with love.
* Imagine the most comfortable writing space in your home.

New Moon Writing Prompts

This would feel *really* good to write over the next few weeks . . .

This feels emotionally important . . .

What's rising up in my heart . . .

This would feel nurturing to my reader . . .

Reflecting on the past few weeks . . .

My inner writer needs more tenderness here . . .

I intend to nurture . . .

My home provides . . .

My words calm . . .

I intend to build . . .

Waxing Moon Actions & Prompts

Waxing Moon Actions

* Tapping into others' emotions is a Cancer skill—make a list of the emotions your ideal clients and readers feel *before* you work with them or write down what attracts them to your words.
* Create a feel-good and nurturing space to get cozy with your words.
* Give yourself permission to write the thing that might make you cry today, and let the tears flow. If they splash on the page, write around them, knowing they carry powerful healing energy.
* Plan a writing retreat for yourself and a few others if you like. It can be as simple and sweet as you desire.
* List five familiar ways you find flow—can you schedule one of them this week?
* Take time to process any emotions that come up fully, and honor them before moving through your writing. If you ignore them now, they'll come back even stronger.
* Write or research about your ancestors, your past, and past lives.

Waxing Moon Writing Prompts

My comfort zone . . .

These emotions want to come to the surface . . .

I need to process this fully before moving forward with my writing project . . .

How can I do my thing and feel a sense of internal comfort?

What comforts could be holding me back?

My writing fulfills . . .

Happy writing . . .

My dream writing space is here now . . .

Writing near the water . . .

I intend to be disciplined about . . .

Full Moon Actions & Prompts

Full Moon Actions

* Review your list of unfinished projects and decide what needs to be prioritized and what needs to fall away.
* Reconnect with a past client or your email list. Connect without an agenda, only to truly check in and see how they're doing and if you can be of service to them in any way.
* Revisit a favorite old book or a piece of writing. Ask it, "What do I need to know?"

* As you finalize your writing and are unsure if it's ready to publish, ask yourself these four questions: 1) Is it good for me? 2) Is it good for the people I love? 3) Is it good for my community and readers? 4) Is it good for everyone? Answering yes to just the first one is all you need. The others are bonuses.
* Tweak your bios or about page, sprinkling in some emotional words.

Full Moon Writing Prompts

What no longer feels aligned and wants to be let go?

This feels emotionally important . . .

Writing fast . . .

My higher self wants to flow with . . .

I'll no longer nurture . . .

I'm grateful for the security . . .

I'll stop micromanaging . . .

I'm thankful I released these fears . . .

Freedom from emotions . . .

I feel blessed . . .

Waning Moon Actions & Prompts

Waning Moon Actions

* Make a list of all your writing projects going on. What can you scrap? What do you want to go deeper on?
* Notice the themes and any emotions that have been bubbling up over the past few weeks.
* Trust you might not have clarity about why something's coming up yet, and you'll know at the next new moon.
* Edit some writing that's familiar to you—it might flow quickly and easily today.
* Nurture your writing practice, making sure the time feels sacred, safe, and quiet.
* Look back through any old journals (that you haven't burned) and celebrate your growth.

Waning Moon Writing Prompts

I'm no longer hiding . . .

I'm dropping the armor around . . .

When I truly listen . . .

I'm open . . .

I'm letting this in . . .

I stay healthy . . .

I feel more peaceful every day . . .

Daily joy . . .

I feel comfortable . . .

I'm so grateful I get to write . . .

LEO

"Put your sunglasses on. I am sunshine."

SUN DATES: July 23 - August 22

SYMBOL: The Lion — throughout history, the majestic lion has symbolized courage, power, and sovereignty. The lion is a strong, noble, and regal leader.

ELEMENT: Fire — the radiance of fire; a sustaining flame that expresses outward

MODE: Fixed — stabilizing and sustaining

ENERGY: Masculine — expressive, confident, and visible

RULING PLANET: The Sun — gives life to everything on Earth and represents our conscious minds and creative energy

HOUSE: Fifth

The Fifth House represents creativity, self-expression, joy, and enjoyment. It's associated with romance, play, artistic creation, and being brave to share your one-of-a-kind voice with the world.

BODY PARTS: heart, middle back

PAIR: Aquarius

METAL: Gold — purity, perfection, vitality, and prosperity

GEM: *Ruby*: vitality, passion, and energy

COLORS:

Gold: confidence, authority, vitality

Purple: creativity, luxury, power

Red: passion, courage, loyalty, devotion

Orange: energy, enthusiasm, courage

Yellow: joy, optimism, clarity

FLOWERS:

Sunflower: vitality, admiration, strength, positivity

Gerbera: happiness

Marigold: passion

ESSENTIAL OILS:

Sweet Orange: relaxation and happiness

Grapefruit: positivity and energy, mood boosting, clarity

Lime: uplifting mood

Lemongrass: rejuvenating

Geranium: emotional balance, confidence, compassion, and understanding

Myrrh: grounding

Frankincense: peace, relaxation, and overall wellness

MANTRAS:

I will.
I am.
I shine.

KEYWORDS:

active, asset, authoritative, bold, caring, cheerful, committed, confidence, dignified, drama, express, focused, fun, gamble, generous, gorgeous, hospitable, identity, image, innocence, joy, loving, mask, noble, originality, performance, persevering, presence, pride, privilege, promote, radiant, regal, remarkable, romance, royal, self-expression, shine, smile, sovereign, stage, star, stubborn, success, talent, theater, VIP, visibility, warm, yourself

CONTENT INSPIRATION:

planning, dreaming, and doing BOLD things that feel like big love • tapping into your authentic self and voice • stoking the tiny sparks inside that have been calling you to go to the next level • planning the rest of the year • making art • indulging in style • playing • being bold • leading • embracing glamour • shining a light

WRITING WITH THIS SIGN:

You probably know some Leos who command a room with confident charisma as if they're not even trying—the ones who walk into a party and seem to already know everyone. They're effortlessly magnetic, and everyone remembers their name. You might think they're extroverted, though they may very well not be. Some have a literal stage, but others make their own stage—elaborate meals on holidays, on the field or court of their sport, on the page.

Leo needs to shine and be fully seen. If your words are feeling anything but shiny and happy, explore what other areas of your life might be feeling dull. If you're not looking after your health, for instance, you might be ignoring your relationships or watching crappy television instead of reading books or engaging in activities that will nourish your mind.

Are you truly enjoying your writing project? Can you feel from the bottom of your heart that you love your work in progress? If you answered no to both of these questions, see where you can shift this with Leo's warming energy. Maybe your writing project needs more from you—ask it what it needs. Spend some time journaling on what you're currently feeling about your project without forcing answers. See what comes up and make shifts where you can to move the stagnant energy.

Consider where you can move into a natural leadership position and become a prominent thought leader with your words—whether spoken, written, or both. Writing assertively, concisely, and confidently, say what needs to be said. This might even be the thing that others are afraid to say out loud. Just make sure you're speaking in the right arena so you stand out in the right crowd.

Like the sun, Leo shares warmth generously. The sun isn't just for a select few—it's for whoever is seeking the pure, divine light. Writing from a loving place, aiming to help those in need and be in service, is always oh, so Leo.

Express your creativity with your words without trying to be overly clever. There's an expressive and even a spicy quality here—the need to make, create, and keep the channel open so you can express authentically without ego.

Challenge yourself to set ambitious writing goals every month, quarter, and year. Let those writing goals be unrealistic to everyone else as you move forward one step at a time with unwavering trust in yourself.

HIGH-VIBE LEO: Fully trusting your intuition and leading with a balance of integrity, charm, and strength. Your writing is a lighthouse that shines for those who need it. Your words *want* to be read. Prioritize pleasure as you write.

LOW-VIBE LEO: Writing or speaking to be overly persuasive and power-hungry. Turning to drama or attention-seeking at all costs. Stay mindful of seeking too much external flattery, which can lead you to neglect your intuitive nudges. Writing for validation, or writing to perform instead of writing authentically from the heart. Lighten up and detach a little with Aquarius energy.

Nourishing Body, Mind, Spirit

BODY: Eat bright, sunshiny foods—yellow, red, and orange peppers, zucchini flowers, and sunflower seeds. Indulge in some heart-opening cacao or dark chocolate. Move your body in strong, confident ways.

MIND: Try something new, find flow in a new challenge, or channel your determination into an act of service.

SPIRIT: Trust your full, bright expression, sharing your light no matter what you're writing.

New Moon Actions & Prompts

New Moon Actions

- Keep your emotions out of the way of your writing. You might write from a neutral place today. Let it flow.
- See this time as one of rebirth when we're given a chance to start fresh.
- Set your intentions for writing with words like, "I'm so happy and grateful that I easily drafted my book by [date]. Bringing it to life with joy, abundance, and expansion. Thank you, thank you, thank you."
- Commit to personal goals that express the high-vibing energies of the lion.
- Boost your self-confidence by discovering your path as a distinct individual, and express yourself boldly in writing.
- Uncover your unique creative writing gifts and weave them into whatever you write.
- Plan your next launch with all the bold details, including how you'll celebrate.
- Trust your intentions are true *while* you enjoy the writing process.
- As you prepare to write, feel enjoyment, happiness, and a glow in your heart.

New Moon Writing Prompts

I radiate . . .

I'm called to go big . . .

A loving expression would be . . .

My higher self wants to shine . . .

I am warm . . .

The confident writer shows up . . .

Writing this is exciting . . .

I'm in love with writing . . .

I create the writing life I want . . .

My greatest asset . . .

Waxing Moon Actions & Prompts

Waxing Moon Actions

* Tap into Leo's generous spirit and write online reviews for businesses you love, local restaurants you frequent, service providers you had a good experience with, and books you've recently enjoyed.
* Write any necessary communication to others in a more personal, caring, and loving manner.
* If you're writing a blog, book chapter, or email, imagine you're writing to one person, not the masses.

* Wear bright colors, any color that resembles fire, or a deep purple, like the royalty you are.
* Make pleasure a priority during your writing today and throughout the rest of your day, beyond your desk.
* Light extra candles.
* Swap your light bulbs from blue or white to amber or red (also better for your eyes after sundown, which might make for better sleep).
* Move through your day with complete confidence in everything you do.
* Write your draft with full permission to let the intensity come through—whether it's love, anger, or joy, feel it deeply and use the emotions as fuel. Now, if you write an angry draft, let it sit and come back to it during a waning moon. You might find opportunities later to adjust the language so that the angry emotions in the message don't muddy it.
* Reach out to people to plant seeds, and let the extra visibility boost your momentum.

Waxing Moon Writing Prompts

A big yellow spotlight is shining on . . .

I need to bring this through . . .

I love . . .

With full confidence, I can . . .

I lead . . .

My inner children need play . . .

This is getting brighter . . .

Golden . . .

My words attract . . .

Visibility on the writing I love provides . . .

Full Moon Actions & Prompts

Full Moon Actions

* Write with warmth. Feel the warmth of your words in your heart space as you let them out.
* Give all of your intentions to write, being fully present, all in with a fiery focus at the page.
* Encourage yourself through a fun challenge or try something new—a new writing style, writing with a new pen, or writing in a place you normally wouldn't.
* Push your body to your personal max, choose the heavier dumbbell, or go for a personal fitness record (safely).
* Make sure to move your body, as you may find it challenging to write otherwise. If you feel antsy and agitated at the page, move the energy first and see where you might be letting stagnant energy stick around.
* Reach out to current and past clients to request testimonials or reviews.

* Because the loyal Leo might not know when to drop a writing project out of pride, revisit your intentions for writing the piece in the first place—and drop it if it no longer lights you up.
* Celebrate the actions you've taken so far.
* Launch your new project or make public announcements to let your work shine in the world.

Full Moon Writing Prompts

This was recently illuminated . . .

This needs to fall away . . .

The highest, most aligned expression of my creativity looks like . . .

The sun melts this stuckness away . . .

I'm calling in . . .

I'm taking risks . . .

I see this skyrocketing . . .

Every day, I write what I want . . .

How lucky am I . . .

I'm awesome . . .

Waning Moon Actions & Prompts

Waning Moon Actions

* While you're editing, see where you can weave Leo's qualities and keywords into your writing.
* Notice which sections of your writing need some more love and attention.
* See where you can shine more generously.
* Add a layer of excitement to your writing. As you edit, notice if you tried to muffle your innate excitement. Use a thesaurus and play with words like exciting, exhilarating, and thrilling.
* Find your unique expression of joy in the editing process.
* If you're asking for external feedback, testimonials, or book reviews, ground yourself first to trust your innate worth.
* Let go of any validation-seeking and insecurities around being seen.
* If you find yourself in an editing flow when you're interrupted and want to keep writing, find a way to let go of any frustration quickly.
* Play with something creative and consider making art outside of the page. Think of it as an exercise in creative cross-training and filling the creative well.

Waning Moon Writing Prompts

I allow love . . .

I'm excited for . . .

My unique expression . . .

I'm loyal to . . .

I'm emerging from behind the scenes . . .

The rose-colored glasses are coming off . . .

Since I realized____, I'm so great at writing . . .

I love this writing life . . .

I'm confident in my writing . . .

My writing fuels my transformation . . .

VIRGO

"I'm here to make everything better."

SUN DATES: August 23 - September 22

SYMBOL: The Maiden/Virgin — a woman carrying a sheaf of wisdom, representing the harvesting of wheat at the time of year of the Virgo (late summer)

ELEMENT: Earth — the refinement of earth; imagine a flower or herbs

MODE: Mutable — adjusting, improving, and organizing

ENERGY: Feminine — receptive, analytical, and discerning

RULING PLANET: Mercury — the messenger and ruler of day-to-day communication and expression (also rules Gemini)

HOUSE: Sixth

The Sixth House represents everyday work, routines, and health. It's also about service, habits, organization, and how you sustain physical and mental well-being.

BODY PARTS: small intestine, digestive system, sympathetic nervous system, liver, spleen, pancreas

PAIR: Pisces

METAL: Quicksilver — appears to move and change, is highly reflective, and is associated with the mind's ability to stay fluid and changeable

GEMS:

Sapphire: loyalty and trust

Sardonyx: eloquence

Yellow Agate: memory and logic

Peridot: youthfulness and a connection to nature

COLORS:

Tan/Beige: stability, practicality, grounding

Blue: calm, focus, clarity

Warm Yellow: mental clarity, constructive energy, insight

Gray: discipline, neutrality, organization

FLOWERS:

Morning Glory: love, life, death

Aster: honesty, loyalty, patience

Chrysanthemum: beauty and longevity

ESSENTIAL OILS:

Tea Tree: calming, invigorating, stabilizing

Sandalwood: calming, soothing, warming

Fir: uplifting and calming

Frankincense: balancing and grounding

Patchouli: earthy grounding and stability, sensuality

Vetiver: calming and peaceful

Lavender: soothes anxiety and overwhelm

Eucalyptus: boosts mental energy

Thyme: stimulates concentration, clarity

Clary Sage: relaxes frustration and irritability, balancing

MANTRAS:

I analyze.

I improve.

I think.

KEYWORDS:

analyze, assistant, attentive, competent, daily habits, declutter, delegate, dignified, diligent, duty, earthy, efficient, environment, filter out, function, functional, good fortune, health, helper, holistic, humility, inquisitive, intellectual, intelligent, loved ones, medicine, meticulous, neat and orderly, order, organize, perfect, pure, regulation, responsibility, role, routine, schedule, serve, service, skill, smart, spotless, strengths, teacher, tidying, time, trust, well-being, wholesome

CONTENT INSPIRATION:

content style • content format • how you teach • how you serve • your style • health—upgrading routines and systems, habits, working out, and eating well • updating systems to make them more efficient • hiring service providers, helpers, and assistants • breaking a big project down into actionable and practical steps • self-improvement • routines

WRITING WITH THIS SIGN:

As an earth sign, we might think of the ground when we consider Virgo. However, just like air and water have differing qualities, so does earth. Virgo is like a tree, flower, or plant—symbolizing nature's delicacy and adaptability.

When the moon is in Virgo, it feels easier to do challenging things; make a list and get ready to feel the immense satisfaction of actually getting through the whole thing. Virgo loves to be productive and get things done, and can tackle the tough writing piece you've been putting off—so follow that vibe today!

Any writing project that felt too emotional to take on is on deck for writing with Virgo. Write or edit the complicated piece—take it apart and put it back together because Virgo takes its curious mind and heart to analyze, sort, group, and make sense of the mess.

Create some structure around your writing time, space, and how you write. Outlining might serve your writing project well. Also, observe and analyze before diving into your writing or editing. Virgo isn't a big risk taker, so see where you want to use some of this methodical energy to be thoughtful in your writing project.

Let go of perfectionism and get quiet. See what the writing needs and approach your writing as an act of service. Ask yourself: "How can I serve these words best?" You might not jump in and start editing right away but rather make some notes first. Then, when you get into the work and are elbows deep, feel how satisfying it is to focus on the details without obsessing over them.

HIGH-VIBE VIRGO: Curiously explores how to make things better and then methodically goes in to improve it—a light touch at first, trusting your expertise. Virgo knows her stuff.

LOW-VIBE VIRGO: Perfectionism, rigidity, overthinking, criticizing, or controlling other people or your writing. Thinking you might never get your project just "right," and no one's review is good enough for you. An overly meticulous writing plan or outline can interfere with Virgo's innate strong gut-sensing abilities.

Nourishing Body, Mind, Spirit

BODY: Look at your well-being routine, including your food and movement to support your writing. A clean body means a clear mind and clear writing. Think about where your well-being needs an upgrade. Plan your meals and exercise for the week ahead and do some batch cooking. Enjoy grounding, earthy foods like russet potatoes and golden beets. Maybe you'll even plan a cleanse, fast, or a short raw vegan detox. Since Virgo rules digestion, use some deep belly breathing to activate the parasympathetic, rest-and-digest state, which can be a challenge for this mental sign.

MIND: Look at your mental habits. Where do they need an upgrade? This is also a good time to make sure you're paying attention to your thoughts. They might sound harsh or more critical during a Virgo moon. Notice them as an observer. Watch your thoughts and sense what you feel in your body. Write down all the sensations, putting a big X across the negative ones and rewriting them as positive statements. Then, take the negative ones and burn, recycle, or tear them up and throw them out.

SPIRIT: Ask to be shown how you can best serve God with your gifts.

New Moon Actions & Prompts

New Moon Actions

* Review your writing routine. Think about where it needs an upgrade.
* Ask your readers, "How can I best serve you today?"
* Look for ways to support your nervous system before, during, and after writing—box breathing (breathe in for a count of four, hold at the top for a count of four, exhale for four, hold again and repeat a few times), grounding or earthing, getting sun, and spending time in nature.
* With order created from an outline or to-do list, prioritize each item so you can review it quickly and efficiently—knowing exactly what to do next and what's coming after. It feels secure to have that structure in place and eliminates decision fatigue because you know what to do next.
* Look at your writing project with a youthful eye and grounded beginner's mind and ask: "What seeds will I plant in the earth for my writing project?"

New Moon Writing Prompts

My well-being . . .

My writing practice nurtures . . .

My words heal . . .

I'm solving . . .

I'm an expert . . .

I want order . . .

My favorite writing format . . .

I choose what helps me grow . . .

I operate best . . .

When my body is in optimal condition . . .

Waxing Moon Actions & Prompts

Waxing Moon Actions

* Pay attention to where you can connect your mind with your body.
* Switch it up—it's okay to change things that aren't working!
* Add some structure to your writing space and your writing process.
* Think about the growing light from the moon shining on the writing efforts and habits you want to grow.

* Write the challenging SFD today, imagining you remove your brain from your head while you write and set it on the desk next to you. Don't worry—you'll get it back later.
* Keep a notebook nearby for all the thoughts—especially the looping ones that drop in today. Write them down so you can stay focused on your project, then revisit your thoughts later.
* Dive into a batch-writing session and focus on a few blog drafts and chapters, or get ahead on drafts of social content or podcast outlines.
* Try the Pomodoro technique—set a 25-minute timer, write without looking until the timer dings, then put it away if you like, or take a five-minute break and dive back in if you're feeling inspired.
* Write about details—it's a great time for that.
* Outline your writing project and create a plan for the week, month, or quarter, giving yourself the structure to know you'll make good progress on it this week.

Waxing Moon Writing Prompts

I serve . . .

My writing project needs this from me . . .

I'm curious . . .

My words help . . .

I'm improving . . .

Good fortune . . .

I write quickly . . .

My authority . . .

The best course of action . . .

My greatest strengths . . .

Full Moon Actions & Prompts

Full Moon Actions

* Stay in the flow with what's going on instead of trying to fight it.
* Review your work from a place of service and ask how you can improve it. Maybe you'll tweak, republish, and reshare on social media.
* Review the writing that felt challenging to write or that you think will be challenging to read. Read it from the perspective of your most loved reader or client, and ask, "Will this serve them?"
* Do a light edit of your work—aim to move quickly and lightly, with the hands of an expert gardener pruning the obvious weeds and fading foliage.
* Use the extra energy from the light in the sky to clean up a big writing file—rearrange, snip, prune (and remember to save anything you cut from your drafts into another file—you might find inspiration there for another day).

* Poke holes in your current writing project and make notes where more research or details will make it stronger.

Full Moon Writing Prompts

Are my current writing projects satisfying?

I let go of perfectionism . . .

Criticism . . .

I'm (becoming) the best in the world at . . .

I quickly adapt . . .

I forgive . . .

I'm dropping attachment . . .

These troubles dissolve . . .

I'm becoming so much more efficient . . .

I'm grateful for . . .

Waning Moon Actions & Prompts

Waning Moon Actions

* Editing to make things just a little bit better might feel good today—so consider making some fast, focused, and efficient edits, even if you're doing a light-touch edit first and noting where you need to add more research or go deeper later.

* After you're finished with the quick round of edits, focus on detail-oriented revisions and challenging edits.
* Explore where you can add another layer of detail to your writing. And even before you do that, read your piece objectively, keeping the critical voice quiet.
* Do the final proof of your website copy or blog post, or the final review of your manuscript before sending it to print.
* Make a massive to-do list of all the things you want to finish before the next new moon, trusting there's a good chance you're going to get through most of it today.
* Clean and organize your writing space, online file storage, and paper files, and purge what's no longer serving you ahead of the new moon.
* Stay fluid and changeable with your drafts. Add feminine grace if you find you need to pivot your writing project, changing quickly like the water.
* Shred old stacks of paper in your office for clearer energy—get rid of what's no longer serving your writing projects.
* See the order in the chaos of your writing project and know the order is in there—you're just going to chisel to get there.
* Go through all your old notes and files. What feels valuable to pay attention to?

Waning Moon Writing Prompts

I no longer compare . . .

I release my writing and it serves . . .

I complete . . .

I've developed patience . . .

The help I need . . .

Only good can come . . .

Thank you . . .

A huge weight has been lifted . . .

Falling away . . .

I'm free to . . .

LIBRA

"I look good and I write well."

SUN DATES: September 23 - October 22

SYMBOL: The Scales — symbolizing justice and fairness, Libra measures and weighs matters carefully, aiming for equality, balance, harmony, and give-and-take

ELEMENT: Air — a steady wind that shapes clouds

MODE: Cardinal — initiating dialogue and relationship

ENERGY: Masculine — outward, relational, connecting points of view

RULING PLANET: Venus — the planet that accentuates creativity and our tastes and pleasures. Other themes include love life, money, and the need for harmony.

HOUSE: Seventh

The Seventh House covers relationships, partnerships, collaboration, and one-on-one connections, including romantic and business partnerships, and the ways we relate to others with balance and harmony.

BODY PARTS: adrenal glands, lower back, kidneys, veins

PAIR: Aries

METAL: Copper — holds enhancing properties and is associated with beauty, love, artistry, and sensuality. Let copper enhance the vibe of your writing space.

GEMS:

Sapphire: wisdom and a calm mind

Smoky Quartz: grounding and connecting to Mother Earth

Jade: prosperity and longevity

Diamond: strength, commitment, endurance

COLORS:

Ivory: balance, harmony, elegance

Pastel Green: calm, renewal, diplomacy

Rose Pink: love, beauty, compassion

Indigo Blue: intuition, fairness, wisdom

FLOWERS:

Rose: love, beauty, passion

Narcissus: inner reflection and inspiration—and on the negative side, vanity

ESSENTIAL OILS:

Rose: love, beauty, sensuality

Geranium: balance

Lavender: calming and balancing

Sandalwood: grounding

Jasmine: connection and intimacy

Neroli: calming and uplifting

MANTRAS:

I relate.
I co-create.
I harmonize.

KEYWORDS:

agreement, attract, balance, beauty, captivate, clever, collaborate, connect, connection, contract, cooperation, elegance, empathy, encounter, etiquette, fair, fairness, fashion, flawless, good taste, grace, harmony, love, manners, partner, peace, relationship, romance, social, sophisticated, soul mate, style, win-win

CONTENT INSPIRATION:

the stuff that's not for you but still on your to-do list • your perfect match in terms of strategic partnerships • business friends • collaborators • luxurious projects • synergies • networking and collaboration opportunities • marriages • contracts • first impressions • nurturing your clients and readers • beauty of your writing space

WRITING WITH THIS SIGN:

See if you felt the shift with the moon moving from Virgo to Libra. It might feel like a welcome change from the effort it takes to manage any inner critic voices you've still got hanging in there. Libra is all about balance, beauty, harmony, peace, cooperation, collaborative style, and grace in relating to each other, like your readers or clients.

Air signs are intellectual, detached, and fair-minded. This detached vibe can make it easier to write the SFD—separating yourself from the outcome and fully surrendering at the page—as long as you can be okay with the draft not looking pretty just yet. Your first drafts might even look more visually appealing during a Libra moon, and in an effortless way, bringing the *je ne sais quoi.*

Libra is other-oriented and focused on partnerships, connections, and collaborations. Do you need a partner to help bring your writing into the world? Would an accountability buddy help bring your writing project to life?

Some might accuse Libra of being flighty—but if the project doesn't bring a sense of balance, they could flit away.

Libra aims for harmony and equality, is artistic, and has a keen sense of balance and an eye for attractiveness. Libra achieves its goals through the powers of attraction and diplomacy. This is a great time to write the things that require just the right amount of grace, elegance, and tact.

HIGH-VIBE LIBRA: Going deep with another, connecting one-on-one with your readers, going with the flow, and finding beauty and peace in all situations. Creating harmony among the chaos. Finding pleasure in the sweet spot between a productive writing practice and feeling good while writing.

LOW-VIBE LIBRA: Doing everything for others first and not looking after your own needs. This can look like people-pleasing, avoiding conflicts, and having trouble making decisions. It can also look like overthinking your writing and editing, trying to please all your readers and even people who aren't in your audience. Wanting to make sure everyone is fairly represented could lead to procrastination—*I don't want to decide!* You may even display split personalities—your online persona being different from your home life. Also, you may engage in comparison, holding high expectations for your drafts to read like someone's finished writing project.

Nourishing Body, Mind, Spirit

BODY: Frumpy clothes simply won't work for Libra. Invest the extra few minutes in your clothes, accessories, and appearance today. Bring that quiet confidence to the page.

MIND: Since air signs are intellectual, impartial, and fair-minded, use a Libra moon to detach from the outcome of your writing project. Create what you need to create and move on to your next project.

SPIRIT: Like the butterfly, your transformation can unfold with everything you touch turning to gold.

New Moon Actions & Prompts

New Moon Actions

* Find some synergies in your writing. Read over your body of work and stay open to potential combinations of two seemingly unrelated pieces that could complement each other beautifully.

- Curate a vision board of your dreamiest writing retreat.
- Imagine your writing space as the most beautiful it could be.
- List your most trusted business and writing friends. Do they fit where you're going? Is there anyone missing?
- Explore your relationships on and to social media—are you following accounts that make you feel at peace? Do the people you're connected with expand your mind or make you feel contracted or agitated?
- Plant seeds for the beauty your writing will bring to the world, and start planning your action steps—as a cardinal sign, Libra loves action.
- Beautify a project plan or spreadsheet here—indulge and make it shine!

New Moon Writing Prompts

I serve my readers best . . .

I'm craving more balance . . .

I bring peace . . .

I harmonize . . .

Luxury means . . .

My eye for beauty . . .

I'm making over . . .

This is the most sophisticated . . .

Quiet confidence . . .

What if I combined these two things?

Waxing Moon Actions & Prompts

Waxing Moon Actions

* Explore how your clients and readers prefer to be nurtured.
* Add some beauty to your writing space by thinking about sights, sounds, and textures—bring in some fresh flowers, essential oils, and plant life.
* Notice the sights, smells, sounds, and textures of your writing spaces as you move throughout your day.
* Since Libra can illuminate many sides of a situation, use the fast-moving, spring-like energy to do some stream-of-consciousness writing as quickly as possible on all the sides of a story or argument you're about to write.
* Schedule some connection calls or attend networking events. Wrap up every interaction, asking, "What do you need right now?" Or "What support do you need?" Usually, whoever you're talking to will offer the same.
* Visit a museum or art gallery for inspiration.

Waxing Moon Writing Prompts

If I could collaborate with ___, we'd make . . .

My writing practice nurtures . . .

My writing supports my life . . .

The best spot for writing looks like . . .

Writing with grace sounds like . . .

This feels unbalanced (note you may not need to change anything!) . . .

I'm grateful for balance . . .

Beautiful writing looks like . . .

I'm going to go deeper . . .

When I wear . . .

Full Moon Actions & Prompts

Full Moon Actions

* Have you worked with some great people and businesses lately? Leave them a review on their public social profiles and web search sites, and send other clients or customers their way.
* Write a few book reviews for books you've read and enjoyed recently. (I only leave positive reviews. If I didn't enjoy a book, I keep it to myself.)
* Send a handwritten note, a kind email, or a note of thanks via text message. Sprinkling good vibes toward others who have made improvements in your life goes a long way to change someone's day—maybe even their whole life.
* Perform an act of service for someone—unprompted. Note you don't have to tell the world you're doing it.
* Create an online poll or send a client or reader survey.

Full Moon Writing Prompts

I'll make my writing space beautiful today . . .

This task no longer brings peace . . .

This tends to always be out of balance . . .

When I write whatever I want . . .

I smile inside . . .

I said goodbye to people-pleasing . . .

I'm decisive . . .

Thanks to this, I'm no longer stressed . . .

I appreciate the sweetness . . .

I'm giving a toast to . . .

Waning Moon Actions & Prompts

Waning Moon Actions

* Make some small upgrades to your writing. Garnish by adding white space to help the reader move through your story.
* Clean off your desk, toss old papers, donate old books, and switch around your decor to get ready to bring in new energy with the next moon cycle.
* Color code your physical and digital files and delete junk in all your spaces.

* Put your drafts into their final forms, adding pictures that capture the tone you're conveying for blogs, formatting quickly and easily, like an artist.
* Do a round of edits on your piece that include words that spark thoughts of beauty—attractive, charming, stunning, gorgeous, lovely, elegant, pretty, alluring.
* If you feel a pull to get together or have conversations with others, and have trouble deciding whether to do that or not, trust your intuition that the right opportunity will be the one you choose (being alone vs. being with others).
* Tweak your website copy, revisit a popular blog, and update your social bios, balancing the words in each sentence. Some sentences should be short and quick, some a little longer.
* Create appropriate visual breaks when writing a long block of text. Ignore the tendency to try to find a perfect formula (Libra helps with this), and instead, do it intuitively. For instance, if you're looking at a blog and see one line of text, a blank line, and then one line again, that's visually repetitive, and readers can unconsciously skip over it. This is the time to tweak it.
* Weave subheadings into your website copy or blog posts.
* Create images for your social posts or refresh some images on your blogs.
* Reshare old posts on social media. Rework an old graphic and update the caption.

Waning Moon Writing Prompts

My to-do list is out of balance . . .

I lead with grace . . .

This is dull and has to go . . .

I won't be pressured . . .

I could talk all night about this . . .

I'm proud of the action I've taken . . .

Looking at what I've co-created . . .

I no longer spend my time . . .

I made a clean break from . . .

I'm grateful for this favorable circumstance . . .

SCORPIO

"Go deep or go home."

SUN DATES: October 23 - November 21

SYMBOLS: The Scorpion — a symbol of strength, resilience, protection, and power. In old Egyptian and Greek myths, it stands for bravery. Another symbol for Scorpio is the Eagle, which also symbolizes bravery and strength, plus a clear vision and intelligence.

ELEMENT: Water — deep, still like a swamp, and ruled by Mars, the hottest of the water signs

MODE: Fixed — penetrating, focused, and transformative

ENERGY: Feminine — inward and intense

RULING PLANETS: Mars & Pluto

Mars (traditional) expresses energy and passion.

Pluto (modern) represents rebirth and transformation.

HOUSE: Eighth

The Eighth House represents transformation, shared resources, intimacy, and deep emotional bonds. It also covers endings and beginnings and the unseen forces that drive change.

BODY PARTS: genitals, bowels, sweat glands, bladder

PAIR: Taurus

METAL: Iron — connected to power, courage, and protection

GEMS:

Opal: faithfulness and confidence

Blood Red Carnelian: courage, protection, vitality

Ruby: passion, love, courage

Topaz: strength and vibrancy

COLORS:

Deep Red: passion, intensity, power

Gold: authority, transformation, value

Purple: depth, intuition, mystery

Black: mystery, depth, transformation, protection

FLOWERS:

Chrysanthemum: optimism and fidelity

Geranium: purity, innocence, spirituality

Rhododendron (purple): royalty and luxury

ESSENTIAL OILS:

Patchouli: uplifting and grounding back into reality

Frankincense: overcoming overthinking, grounding back into focus when taking on too much of others' emotions or are too deep in your latest project

Ylang Ylang: emerging from soul-searching depths while easing stress

Myrrh: encourages spiritual and emotional awakening while grounding back to Earth

Lavender: calming and relaxing

Cedar: transmuting negative energy

Vanilla: warmth and sensuality

MANTRAS:

I transform.

I am powerful.

I am unstoppable.

KEYWORDS:

bond, charisma, comeback, commit, death, deep, destiny, determined, dive, essence, faith, fate, finance, focused, fortune, freedom, hidden, instinct, intense, investment, karma, meditation, merge, money, mysterious, passion, perceptive, possessive, precious, private, prowling, psychological, rare, recharge, reset, resourceful, resolve, resurrection, sex, soul level, strength, transformation, truth, uncompromising, unshakeable, value

CONTENT INSPIRATION:

case studies • sharing what works and is proven • behind-the-scenes or approaches of how things work • commitment and going all-in • head-down and focused work • building trust • positioning yourself as an expert • sharing secrets • going deep (no surface-level stuff here) • spicy language • what motivates your creativity and work • unconscious habits

WRITING WITH THIS SIGN:

Scorpio is here to enjoy the ride of transformation. With the scorpion's tail, it can grab and sting—waking you right up. Where are you ignoring your writing project? Maybe you're being called to go deeper into your writing while up until now, you've been dabbling on the surface. The deep and profound writing could be demanding your attention. What stories or projects are you holding back on? You may want to turn your gaze here before you get pricked.

The eagle also represents Scorpio. Did you know the crow is the only bird that attempts to attack him? The eagle gives zero fudges, though, and lets him peck away at its neck. Instead of turning its majestic head to fight him, he flies *higher,* where eventually, the crow can't handle the lack of oxygen and falls away.

The lesson is to bravely go deeper (higher) than anyone else, fly higher or swim deeper than anyone trying to peck at your neck while you write. Ignore the clowns and trolls, and stay focused on your transformation.

The other symbol for Scorpio is the phoenix, which represents the ultimate, final transformation.

Known for intensity, this is the time to write or edit the things you've been afraid to touch. Scorpio is willing to go there, writing with emotional intensity. Be willing to write the things that were previously private, allow them to transform you, then emerge from the depths.

Scorpio needs action and isn't messing around. Balance the pull to go into the depths with patience to know what you want and trust that you'll grab it at just the right moment (like the quick-moving scorpion). There's no sitting idle thinking about your writing project. Notice the still water with all your senses and jump into the deep end. Be unafraid of creating ripples in the water. No thinking, feeling your way, and going to the depths. Notice the still water surrounding you as you immerse yourself in your inner world of words.

Scorpio themes are typically seen as heavy: money, life, death, resurrection, and sex—not exactly topics that make for small talk. Use a Scorpio moon to *go there.* Scorpio concentrates, evicts, and reforms. If you're writing during Scorpio season, this is a time of deep focus. It's no accident that the intense 30-day writing challenge NaNoWriMo (see the introduction again for why I don't recommend this challenge for women) happens in November, a good chunk of Scorpio season.

Intuitive nudges can be strong here, and if you're floating in a smooth lake, you're more receptive to the spiritual nudges from your higher self, the Divine, God.

It's a dance if we happen to be in Scorpio season and under a Scorpio moon, having that strong-willed emotion of wanting to go deep and feeling hesitation, wondering if you're capable. See if there's a way for you to play with both.

It's a great time to get lost in a creative project. Give yourself permission to go to the depths, being okay with being unsure where you are without trying to control it.

Before you emerge from your transformation cocoon, ask yourself where you might have kept parts of you locked away out of fear of being "too much." When you come up for air to perhaps have some conversations with others and do some human things, see where you can get to know them beyond the surface. In those moments when you're getting to know someone, those sparks might come, especially if you're focused on being still and quiet.

You could start to connect the dots and get other inspiration.

If you ever feel stagnant or monotonous in your work or writing, reach out to a few people in your network and have conversations with those you trust or want to get to know. No agenda. You're not trying to pitch them or convince them of anything. Simply set up a connection call or get out of the house to meet them at a local cafe or bookshop. It's a great way to stay in touch with people and a natural way to share what you're up to.

HIGH-VIBE SCORPIO: Living each day like it's your last. Relishing the ability to see and appreciate all levels of humanity. Having a deep desire to learn and understand at the deepest level. Asking yourself how you're saying YES.

LOW-VIBE SCORPIO: Making messes with no aim or understanding, writing for personal power or ego, obsessing, or being manipulative. Letting emotions control you and then stirring up drama because you're not fulfilling your own need for passion. Holding onto too many writings without publishing some. Scorpio needs some release to allow complete transformation, so if you find yourself in the lower vibe of Scorpio, share a tiny peek of your writing project with someone you trust.

Nourishing Body, Mind, Spirit

BODY: Get in, or be in, the water or near the water and drink lots of water—maybe add some electrolytes. Enjoy seasonal fruits and veggies with a high water content, like watermelon and berries. Notice the area at the base of your spine as you write today. If you're sitting, feel it against the chair before you begin.

MIND: Small talk is out of the question. Stimulate your mind with a book on a fascinating topic—maybe psychology—or ask people deeper questions about their work: "Do you love it?" "How did you get into that work?" "What are you passionate about these days?"

SPIRIT: Do your soul and deep healing work, looking at your shadow but not integrating it; instead, sting it and let it wither and disappear. Or, embodying the eagle, see your shadow from way up in the sky and know that it does not define you.

New Moon Actions & Prompts

New Moon Actions

* Carve out some alone time to be with your words.
* Cancel any cancelable plans to be alone with your emotions and your favorite notebook.
* Dive into your journal pages and be willing to go deep without worrying about how much time or how many pages you fill up.
* See journaling as a nurturing practice today and invest some extra time in those pages.

* Use your willpower to create a new writing habit, and initiate your writing project with passion.
* Focus on planting seeds for the writing that feels emotionally important to you.
* Notice what emotions have been showing up over the past few days. Pay attention as an observer, without judgment. You might write these down too.
* Honor past seasons of transformation that you've emerged from.
* Feel into the transformation you're about to embark on.

New Moon Writing Prompts

A strong desire is coming through . . .

The work that's calling me to put my head down and go deep . . .

What writing project feels emotional, like it needs my attention?

I'm planting seeds in the dark soil . . .

I'm courageous . . .

My soul wants to feel . . .

I want to go deeper into . . .

This feels like an invitation to transform . . .

What challenges are coming up?

What do stillness and depth mean for me in my writing?

Waxing Moon Actions & Prompts

Waxing Moon Actions

* Make time on your calendar for deep focus.
* Flow with the writing that feels more passionate, where you can find richer depth, and as you're writing, really *feel* your body as you release the words.
* If you sense you're forcing the words, imagine a deep, quiet lake and notice how the water moves. Write like that water.
* Schedule conversations with people in adjacent industries or with similar interests.
* Do the emotional writing that takes courage to come to the page in a fast, focused, and surrendered draft.
* If you write with lots of emotion, let it come out. No holding back. This is the time for fast drafts without judging. You'll reel it in and ground the writing later. Don't worry about the state it's in—your job is only to show up and let the words flow.

Waxing Moon Writing Prompts

I'm hesitant about writing this . . .

I have some worries this is going to be too much . . . and I let them go . . .

I have fear around sharing about . . .

When I lose track of time . . .

Five things I love doing that I could do for hours . . . (can I schedule one of those things to happen this week?)

I didn't expect this . . .

I might be trying to control the process here . . .

I notice where I'm trying to control my reader . . .

My comeback . . .

My rebirth . . .

Full Moon Actions & Prompts

Full Moon Actions

* Write a fast and spicy draft. Use the words that make you feel punchy or sassy.
* Write about things you've never shared before. You don't have to share it, but writing it can be healing and illuminating.
* Share something vulnerable publicly if it feels right to you.
* Send the slightly intimidating podcast pitch, book proposal, collaboration request, or guest article submission.
* Record audios and use the transcription to serve as the foundation for your writing.
* Ask your audience for something—to leave a comment, answer a deep question, reply to your email, or rate or review your book.

* Take branding photos for your website.
* Record videos and take photos of your favorite things like your bookshelves, favorite coffee nook, a well-loved mug to use in blogs and newsletters.
* Trust that there's some hidden treasure lurking in the depths of your psyche—see what you can uncover.
* Pay attention to what's activating you because there's something for you to see, release, and alchemize.
* Strong determination, especially inner determination, can fuel your writing project around this time.
* Notice if you're trying to apply too much structure to your writing and where that could be making you feel stuck.
* Pay attention to what feels frustrating—if the words don't sound the way you "want" as you write, let them be and see where you can surrender and come back later. Maybe you had the right words the first time. As you write your fast drafts, simply highlight or bold these words, or add a comment in your document to come back to these parts.

Full Moon Writing Prompts

I've learned this about myself, my writing habits, and my practices over the past few weeks . . .

I need to see . . .

This has to go so I can commit . . .

I can put myself out there (even if it feels scary) just to see what happens . . .

I'm feeling triggered by . . .

I might be trying to control my writing too much here . . .

Where am I craving more structure?

I feel like needing to know all the answers to ___ could be slowing me down.

I wrote this in a flow state . . . Revisit that writing and see if you can tap into the flow you found there.

If this piece of writing was my very last . . .

In a past life . . .

Waning Moon Actions & Prompts

Waning Moon Actions

* Get your hands dirty and dive into editing a complicated writing piece. FEEL your way instead of trying to think your way there.
* Do an emotional edit, sprinkling in words from the Scorpio themes and keywords earlier in this section.
* Use images to help you find powerful words by doing an internet search for the emotions you're looking to include in your writing.
* There's no rule for how much emotion to weave into your writing. Emotion helps give your work personality. Use your intuition based on your writing topic and what the reader might expect.

- As you're exploring emotional words to add to your writing, notice if the same or similar sentiments or emotions come out. For example, have you said "excited" eighteen times in one blog? Use an online thesaurus to uncover other words to give you some variety.
- Balance big-picture thinking with going deep. You might go deep in lots of places, or you might go wider or take a 10,000-foot view. See what's coming up for you with your writing, and as you're getting in there and doing some edits.
- Add in the original word you wanted to use when you might have worried it was too much or too strong. Release any beliefs you may have acquired in childhood around being too much.
- Update language that's soft because you're trying to please everyone. Write the authentic truth.
- If you edited as you were writing and censored yourself, add yourself back in.
- Focus, finish, and complete, being confident you'll go deep and get it done.

Waning Moon Writing Prompts

Transformation is happening as we near the end of the moon cycle. This writing practice or writing project needs to go . . .

I can look deeper at my writing . . .

My writing practice would feel more genuine . . .

To balance the big picture with going deep . . .

I'm probably holding back here . . .

What I really want to say is . . .

Does this sound like how I speak?

Am I being fully, completely myself in my writing?

What challenges have come up over the last couple of days?

Looking at my list of writing projects, am I writing them because I want to or do I feel I have to?

SAGITTARIUS

"Lighten up! Let's play!"

SUN DATES: November 22 - December 21

SYMBOL: The Archer — the Sagittarian symbol resembles an arrow, which symbolizes the desire for direction, a higher purpose, and abundance. Notice how it's pointed upward, representing the eternal quest.

ELEMENT: Fire — the expansion of fire, which, like a wildfire, spreads ideas, philosophies, and meaning

MODE: Mutable — expanding, exploring, seeking truth

ENERGY: Masculine — outward, philosophical, big-picture

RULING PLANET: Jupiter — symbolizes reach, broader purpose, and possibilities. The first of the social planets, Jupiter is a moral, just, and truth-seeking force. It looks for insight through knowledge and stays optimistic and growth-oriented (both mental and spiritual). Jupiter is also associated with a sense of humor, goodwill, and mercy.

HOUSE: Ninth

The Ninth House represents expansion, exploration, and higher learning. It also covers philosophy, travel, adventure, teaching, and the pursuit of wisdom or life purpose.

BODY PARTS: hips, thighs, femur, butt

PAIR: Gemini

METAL: Tin — representing knowledge, wisdom, balance, philosophy, mediation, and prosperity

GEMS:

Azurite: clarity, quicker decision-making

Blue sapphire: clear speaking, fearlessness, mental clarity, writing with integrity, boosting concentration and communication skills

Blue Topaz: peace, relaxation, happiness

COLORS:

Orange & Dark Yellow: adventure, luck, positivity, motivation

Deep Purple: creativity, royalty, higher thinking, wisdom

Royal Blue: expansion and wisdom

Deep Turquoise: calm, wisdom, good luck, joy, intuition

FLOWERS:

Carnation: good luck and pure love

Hydrangea: earnestness, prosperity, abundance

Peony: honor and abundance

ESSENTIAL OILS:

Tea Tree: relieves stress and anxiety

Clary Sage: focus, clarity, concentration

Bergamot: eases tension to help be authentic

Lemon: uplifting and brightening

Eucalyptus: invigorating

Chamomile: soothes a busy mind

MANTRAS:

I see.

I dream big.

I explore.

KEYWORDS:

academic, action, adventure, authentic, bold, bright future, carefree, chasing the impossible, communication, curiosity, develop, dive in, dreaming big, ease, expand, extraverted, fearless, fly, focused, fortunate, fortune, frankly, freely, friendly, generous, genuine, goal, grow, inquisitive, inspiration, international, joyful, liberation, luck, media, natural, new world, no mask, open, optimism, outdoors, overseas, positivity, possibilities, publishing, quickly, relaxed, risk, seeking, straightforward, swift, tackle, the unknown, up-front, wander, widen, windfall

CONTENT INSPIRATION:

dreaming big • being a visionary • having optimism and limitlessness • setting up a big vision for next year and beyond • helping your clients see their vision • writing the thing, starting the project, or launching the offer that feels like you're "just going for it" • writing the adventurous blog or chapter that feels fun and expansive, and inviting your reader along for the ride • changing your scenery for writing and editing • sharing your truth • expanding on pieces of writing that already exist • staying centered • expanding possibilities • trying difficult things • overcoming obstacles • embarrassments • flow-building habits

WRITING WITH THIS SIGN:

The switch to a Sagittarius moon can feel like a welcome relief after visiting the deep and serious vibe of Scorpio. It's as if we're picking our heads up from being focused for days and now we get to play. We might look at our writing and sense a seriousness, or it could feel boring. This is the perfect time to inject some fun and levity into your writing projects. Find something light to work with today since you'll be in the mood to wander.

Sagittarius is fire—the kind of blaze that won't be contained and rages on as it pleases, turning anything in its way to ash. Like fire, Sag doesn't do limits, so this is a great time to go huge (bigger than you think!) and do so without any doubt or distractions holding you back. I know a few Sagittarius women who make decisions quicker than anyone. In one case with a book coaching client, when I'd present her with a decision, she'd answer my question before I finished getting it out of my mouth! Make decisions in your writing project like this—from a place of grounded fearlessness and optimism.

We can really tap into Sagittarius's enthusiasm and child-like wonder when we dive into a new—or old—writing project. Maybe you'll roll up your sleeves and play with multiple projects. Sag loves variety—but instead of seeing it as something you need to avoid boredom and therefore picking up too many writing projects and leaving them undone, embrace variety in *one* thing. This might look like relentlessly creating content—videos, free guides, blogs, or social content around your one big project, like your book, signature offer, or primary service. In short, embrace variety in a way that supports you in finishing your most important projects.

Use this enthusiastic and expansive energy to embody the

archer and take aim—upward, to the moon—in your writing project. You know the saying, "Shoot for the moon, land among the stars,"—choose your target, aim high, and trust that the divine will deliver everything you aim for and even more.

Sagittarius is frank, sincere, honest, and forthcoming—such beautiful and clear energy to write with. A generous, fiery sign, it needs its freedom to thrive. See if you can use this energy to focus on one mission at a time and write with complete freedom. If you have a tendency to censor or filter your voice from years of academic or corporate conditioning, now's the time to burn those limits to the ground and write from the ashes you created.

If you can stay present with the ennui of restlessness and carelessness and embrace it with a strong and powerful force, you can use this fire to focus and get the important stuff done.

HIGH-VIBE SAGITTARIUS: Optimistic, excited, limitless, and ready to go for it—and having fun throughout the whole process. Confidently speaking the truth, writing the thing that just might lead you to your truth, and then going right back to loving life.

LOW-VIBE SAGITTARIUS: Overcommitting, overdoing, and irresponsible excess can come as a result of saying yes to too many things because they sounded fun at the time, later realizing you've got more important (or even more exciting) things to do. If you notice this, bring energy from Sagittarius's airy pair, Gemini, and talk about your writing with your writing group and others you trust.

Nourishing Body, Mind, Spirit

BODY: Move that big energy in a fun way. How did you like to move your body as a kid? See if you can walk, run, rollerblade, throw a ball or frisbee, and play in the way you used to before you got so dang serious. Getting outside, soaking in nature's wisdom, and prioritizing a walk with intention might feel good too. Choose a focus (e.g., make a decision about your business or choose a book title), head out for your walk, and see what happens. Feel free to take a small notebook or your phone with you so you can jot down or talk out your insights. Enjoy some denser and heavier whole foods to help with grounding, such as nuts, seeds, or avocado.

MIND: Explore a familiar topic in a new light or from a different angle. Write from a busy place today and strike up a conversation. Leave your earbuds at home to invite in an unexpected connection and fun chat. While some might think Sag is a great starter and poor finisher, it may simply be that you're restless and need some variety and physical movement to support your mind.

SPIRIT: Schedule some fun in your calendar for the rest of the month. Planning a creative date with yourself this week to do something other than writing could also bring joy. What can you do that will bring a smile to your face today?

New Moon Actions & Prompts

New Moon Actions

* Plan an opinion piece. You can decide later where (and if) you'll share it.
* Explore where you can break up your routine—whether in your life or in your writing—and try something new and fun.
* Infuse some of that fiery shake-up-the-monotony energy and optimism into your new moon intentions. This could be the moon cycle to go for it. Write them as big as you can go!
* Aim for the highest possible outcome with full optimism that the outcome is already here and stay open to it being even better.
* Review an old list of ideas. Which ones haven't you put into action yet? Explore if the timing is right to move forward with a seed you already planted.
* Could you take your work-in-progress further and expand on or develop what's already there? This could look like turning your blog series into a book or turning your book into an online course.
* Knowing you're limitless, let yourself dream big while staying open to endless opportunities and possibilities.

* If you're thinking about writing a book, a Sagittarius moon could be just the one to plant seeds for success in writing and publishing it.

New Moon Writing Prompts

My writing project is going to . . .

My reader . . .

It's so possible . . .

I see . . .

I shattered all my limits . . .

When my readers finish this, they're going to feel . . .

What areas of my life need more joy?

Where have I been undermining or underestimating myself?

Allow yourself to dream big—what does it look like?

With total freedom, I . . .

Waxing Moon Actions & Prompts

Waxing Moon Actions

* Plan to release your next writing project in a novel way. Explore what would be totally fresh and playful.
* If your writing feels like it's not flowing, it's a little bit sticky or stagnant, or you're just bored, pick up your computer and

go write somewhere else. Even sitting in another spot in your home can do the trick.

* Shake up your morning routine. Maybe you'll write first and hit the gym later. Maybe you'll work from a cafe or library. Maybe you'll work out at the gym, pack your laptop, and work in the lobby when you're done.
* Brainstorm and draft fun social posts, fresh writing projects, people to connect and collaborate with, new graphics, a new website vibe, or branding.
* Create your vision for the coming year. Then five years from now. Move through your day as if it's here and real today—because it is! There's no need to wait for January 1, the first of the month, or the start of Aries season—start now!
* Break up the routine, and embrace the spontaneous and new. Newness is medicine to disrupt monotony.

Waxing Moon Writing Prompts

It's go time . . .

It's time for adventure . . .

I've been too serious . . .

This project will help my client/reader . . .

I see . . .

I love sharing this wisdom . . .

Where can I take three new risks in my business or writing?

I expand . . .

This is developing . . .

If I could write anywhere in the world . . .

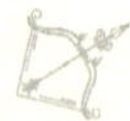

Full Moon Actions & Prompts

Full Moon Actions

* Send the bold story or podcast pitches to some big names.
* Contact potential collaborators or plan an event.
* Go for it and go big.
* Get outside and get your bare feet on the ground.
* Move your energy in a new way or go for a long hike or walk.
* Stay present and optimistic.
* Speak truth no matter what.
* Do the light writing first—maybe you'll only play with the fun writing today.
* Try writing while moving—walking with a notebook and pen on hand (carefully) or recording a voice memo on your phone.
* Make a feel-good writing playlist.
* Let some humor shine through in your writing.
* Find your flow. Have a flow day where you work from lots of places.
* Trust that it's all going according to plan.

- Notice the synchronicities that have popped up since the new moon.

Full Moon Writing Prompts

I'm splurging on . . .

I know this for sure . . .

I'm fired up . . .

It's time to switch things up . . .

I see the bigger picture . . .

I've taken these risks recently . . .

I prioritize hope . . .

Freedom . . .

It would be an adventure to . . .

I'm so fortunate . . .

Waning Moon Actions & Prompts

Waning Moon Actions

- Start thinking of the bigger picture, beyond the current moon cycle, month, calendar, or astrological year (Aries to Pisces). What opportunities can you imagine?
- Write while trusting that your words will serve readers for years.

* Let yourself dream big and enjoy every minute.
* Do a "personality edit" on your writing and add a layer of sneaky fun or cheekiness to your current project, making sure your authentic voice is in there. Maybe you can even dial up the heat on your voice and make it burn brighter.
* Read your writing aloud and notice if it sounds like you. Are you using words you'd normally use? Are you performing in your writing or being truly yourself?
* Review your writing habits and even your lifestyle habits that support your good fortune in writing. Where can you make a shift or change?

Waning Moon Writing Prompts

I'm shedding and releasing this so I can grow bigger and expand in the coming weeks, months, and years . . .

What would my dream look like if I just went for it?

When this project is done, I'm going to celebrate by . . .

My authentic voice . . .

Relaxed . . .

With ease . . .

It's natural . . .

Boldly . . .

My open mind . . .

I complete . . .

CAPRICORN

"Slow and steady — I am determined."

SUN DATES: December 22 - January 19

SYMBOL: The Goat — mountain goats find security in cliffs and heights, the highest places that can be climbed

ELEMENT: Earth — the structure of earth, like the long-term structure of a mountain

MODE: Cardinal — initiating ambition and long-term work

ENERGY: Feminine — inwardly disciplined and strategic

RULING PLANET: Saturn — leaning toward structure and making meaning

HOUSE: Tenth

The Tenth House covers career, reputation, and public life. It rules authority, achievements, long-term goals, leadership, and how you're seen in the world.

BODY PARTS: knees, bones, teeth, joints, skin

PAIR: Cancer

METAL: Lead — representing durability, strength, endurance, and stability

GEMS:

Onyx: self-control, discipline, spiritual strength, and focus

Amber: wisdom and clarity

COLORS:

Brown: grounding, dependability, simplicity

Gray: discipline, structure, neutrality

Black: authority, power, sophistication

Deep Green: ambition, persistence, growth

FLOWERS:

Pansy: consideration, carefulness, pondering

Lotus: patience and faithfulness

ESSENTIAL OILS:

Ginger: eases stress and overwhelm

Peppermint: helps to feel invigorated and refreshed through busy days

Lime: supports positive emotions and gives an energy boost

Wintergreen: helps with mental and emotional fatigue

Vetiver: calming and grounding

Sandalwood: reduces anxiety and stress

MANTRAS:

I achieve.

I contribute.

I use.

KEYWORDS:

advance, ambitious, analyze, assistant, authority, award, background, chosen, commitment, conservative, consistent, constant, discipline, distinguished, down to earth, duty, efficient, formality, foundation, growth, hard work, honest, improvement, long-term goals, master, methodical, official, organize, patience, perfection, planner, position, prudent, public, raise, regulation, resourceful, responsibility, results, rightfully, role, routine, schedule, sincere, skill, social, status, structure, success, tenacity, tidying, top-level, tradition, training, wise, work

CONTENT INSPIRATION:

taking those big dreams and putting them into a structured plan • sharing structured how-tos and instructions for your readers • repurposing of existing content • sharing how to organize ideas and plans with your readers or clients • positioning yourself as the authority on your subject matter by sharing client stories and your wisdom • setting goals • getting organized • reconnecting with people you appreciate • seeking a mentor • elevating your professionalism • boosting your brand and personal recognition • focusing on mastery

WRITING WITH THIS SIGN:

Capricorn is great at slow, determined, and focused movement, checking things off a list with steady tenacity. Be useful and productive all in the name of achieving a desired result—one that will feel satisfying when you reach it.

Try constructing some strong boundaries around your sacred writing time, knowing your responsibilities and commitments, and then get going. There's no need to waste even a second overthinking today. Use that diligent self-control to check the practical writing and editing tasks off your list; perhaps these are the things you've been putting off because you simply didn't want to do them. Capricorn helps you get this done and it'll feel oh-so-pleasing when you do.

Tap into Capricorn's high expectations of themselves. That no-nonsense, all-business sense can support you in being productive and grounded today. Cap's a no-fluff badass.

Capricorn can tackle the tough writing projects one step at a time, looking only at the next step—not the whole staircase. If you're standing at sea level looking up at the top of the mountain thinking, *How will I ever get there?*, that could be overwhelming. Instead, trust your strength, sturdiness, agility, and adaptability, knowing you'll get there, and that it's okay if you change your course along the way.

You might go slower compared to others (so hopefully you're not comparing yourself to others), but you know you *will* arrive at the top. And if you encounter any challenges along the way, look to your foundation—your writing space, practices, and nutrition.

HIGH-VIBE CAPRICORN: Organized, connected, and action-focused, with a strong and clear vision grounded in practicality. Has strong boundaries around writing time and creative energy. With good boundaries, you give yourself a stable and sustainable home for writing ideas to gain structure and develop further.

LOW-VIBE CAPRICORN: Wanting more things for the sake of having them, and getting lost in the weeds of wanting everything to be just right. Believing writing needs to be linear and not trusting the process. Expectations can be so high that you might spin, get overwhelmed, and find yourself lost without taking any action. Watch for all business and no fun. You could reach the end of your day and notice the inner critic getting loud, as if you didn't do enough. Remember, you're doing enough, and you are enough.

Nourishing Body, Mind, Spirit

BODY: Take the time to do something nurturing for your body, like savoring a slow, challenging yoga session, a long walk, a bath, or a massage. Notice and appreciate the support of your knees. Remember to schedule breaks!

MIND: Manage your mind when something feels difficult. See the big picture, and trust you only need to know the next step. You can do this!

SPIRIT: Before embarking on your writing journey, ask yourself if you're climbing the right mountain.

New Moon Actions & Prompts

New Moon Actions

* Plant seeds to find a strong mentor who's been where you want to go or is there now.

* Model your writing practice or habits after someone who does lots of practical things.
* Set intentions for useful things, such as foundational writing pieces.
* Write functional things to warm up to your writing practice—important emails, how-to guides, letters to create change, invitations to connect.
* Choose a writing goal for the next moon cycle—maybe one that felt too large to tackle before.
* Let your guard down and be vulnerable in the safety of your journal pages.

New Moon Writing Prompts

These tasks are actually "shoulds" and can come off my list . . .

These things make me feel safe, secure, and at peace . . .

These writing practices are my tried and true . . .

I take care of things . . .

I'm purposeful about . . .

My goals . . .

I'm the boss . . .

I'm responsible . . .

I do these things well . . .

My plans . . .

Waxing Moon Actions & Prompts

Waxing Moon Actions

* Tidy your workspace and organize any loose papers so you can focus.
* To stay focused when your mind might be flooded with all the ideas, make a big to-do list, then choose just one to three things you can reasonably get done today.
* As a cardinal sign, Capricorn is an action taker. Start drafting the challenging piece you've been procrastinating on.
* Create a 12-week writing plan for yourself.
* Plan one big project or make plans for a bunch of projects.
* If you're up for it, plan the rest of your year.
* As you make progress with your drafts, trust the process.
* If you have the sneaking suspicion that what you're writing doesn't make sense, there's something more useful for you to work on, or you see a better direction, trust that nudge and switch to something else.
* Put the impractical, dreamy writing aside and write practical things that will move your business forward.
* Depending on how you naturally write, you might look at the words and think they feel flat or boring. Leave it alone for now. Come back to them when the moon is in a water sign to add in some emotion.

Waxing Moon Writing Prompts

My priority . . .

When I finish this project, I will . . .

When I follow this plan, I'll . . .

I need to trust . . .

This isn't practical . . .

I take charge . . .

I trust my strength . . .

I'm wiser now . . .

I will strengthen . . .

I receive . . .

Full Moon Actions & Prompts

Full Moon Actions

* Balance the energy of the full moon with grounding practices like yoga, getting outside in the sun, putting your feet on the ground, and eating plenty of raw fruits and veggies.
* Move your body before you focus on your project, knowing that with so much fast-moving outside energy from the full moon, it could feel frenetic, leaving you feeling anxious or stuck in your head.

* Notice what's showing up and see how you might change your plans.
* Take those big dreams and write a giant to-do list. Then, plot out when you'll take action on these items. If you've got a big list of tasks in front of you today, remember to take a breather, look up from the page as much as you can, and schedule something easy or restorative later today.
* Review your writing plans or work-in-progress and see where it needs an infusion of practicality. Does your plan need to come down to earth? If you made your plan during a younger sign like Aries, with the just-go-for-it energy, it might be time to revisit it.

Full Moon Writing Prompts

I'm proud of successfully navigating this transformation . . .

The writing that really resonates with my audience . . .

I'm ready . . .

I could lighten up here . . .

These feelings are coming from outside me . . .

I release any uncertainty around . . .

I eliminate everything unnecessary . . .

Quitting . . .

This is dull and has to go . . .

My effort paid off . . .

Waning Moon Actions & Prompts

Waning Moon Actions

* Focus on getting things done and the satisfaction of crossing those momentous tasks off your list—you're doing it!
* Stay mindful of not overdoing it with a waning moon. It's time to wind down and move a little slower. This could feel stronger as the new moon approaches.
* Since Capricorn is a curiously complicated sign, see if you can channel this energy into editing something that feels complex today.
* Take a hefty piece of writing that might be unnecessarily long and pare it down with shorter sentences and quicker paragraphs.
* Cut out pieces quickly, without emotion or feeling attached to any of the writing.
* If you delete anything from your working drafts, save it to another document and plan to revisit it.
* Bring order to a piece of writing that feels chaotic.

Waning Moon Writing Prompts

I'm being overly judgmental . . .

I could use more discernment here . . .

I could finish this writing project if . . .

I can uncomplicate this . . .

I'm ready to bring more order into . . .

I let go of anxiety . . .

The longer it takes . . .

Beyond all my expectations . . .

Multiplied . . .

I see success . . .

AQUARIUS

"I've got a great idea!"

SUN DATES: January 20 - February 18

SYMBOL: The Water Bearer — even though the symbol for Aquarius is the water bearer, it's an air sign. Just as the water bearer symbolically gives life to the Earth, imagine the abundance of water being poured into your writing work. Ideas flow like a never-ending well of inspiration. Water cleans and clears the past, making way for a fresh, new start. Ever notice how cleansing a good rain feels?

ELEMENT: Air — high-altitude air, stabilizing ideas into systems that shape the future

MODE: Fixed — stabilized, innovative thinking

ENERGY: Masculine — outward, intellectual, progressive

RULING PLANETS: Saturn & Uranus

Saturn (traditional) adds structure and meaning to our world through its strong awareness of the limits of time and matter—definition, rules, boundaries, responsibilities, commitments.

Uranus (modern) inspires enlightenment, progressiveness, objectivity, novelty, and ingenuity. It represents the spark of intuition that spurs invention.

HOUSE: Eleventh

The Eleventh House highlights society, friendships, and collective vision. It's associated with networks, collaboration, shared goals, and the hopes and dreams you pursue with others.

BODY PARTS: ankles, calves, circulation

PAIR: Leo

METAL: Uranium — shape-shifting and awakening properties

GEMS:

Garnet: spiritual grounding, attracting better health, good humor

Amethyst: healing properties

COLORS:

Aqua: balance, serenity, clarity, open communication

Blue: peace, trust, stability, support in speaking truth

Silver: reflection, intuition, mystery, grace

FLOWERS:

Orchid: refinement, unusualness, fertility

Gladiolus: integrity and strength of character

ESSENTIAL OILS:

Ginger: balancing, centering, mental fatigue

Neroli: easing stress and uplifting the mind and mood

Cinnamon: creativity, concentration, warming

Rosemary: strengthening and quick-thinking mental energy

Chamomile: comforting

Black pepper: spicing up and warming to energize the mind

Cedarwood: boosts focus and eases tension

Clove: overcoming negativity and calming the mind

MANTRAS:

I know.
My inspiration is unlimited.
What I offer is unique.

KEYWORDS:

adopt, astrology, astronomy, assertive, break, breakthrough, collaboration, cool, detached, dramatic, eccentric, extraordinary, freedom, freelancing, friendly, futuristic, global, group, humanitarian, idealistic, independent, individualistic, ingenuity, innovate, inspired, intellectual, opinionated, original, planet, programming, progressive, reform, reshape, revolution, scientist, simplify, social justice, social media, streamline, systems, technology, unique, volunteer

CONTENT INSPIRATION:

creating the right offer for your prospective client (their dream solution) • pushing boundaries • making something new—content, product, or through a new medium • breaking through the status quo to take your writing to the next level • looking outside yourself and your industry to think outside the box • inner purpose • sense of community • serving humanity • calling others to join in and share • exploring new tech and tools (hold the generative AI for writing, please) • breaking out of (and throwing away) any box you put yourself in • allowing for full, creative expression • connecting with your community • making the world a better place

WRITING WITH THIS SIGN:

Aquarius is a cool, calm, and collected air sign. With its head in the air, it's rebellious, thinking, "I'm just gonna do what I'm gonna do," and "I'm going for it!" Take that big vision and go after it.

Aquarius looks to the future and is focused on growth—how will you grow as a human through your writing? How can sharing your ideas help the collective growth? Aquarians are also excellent at passing on knowledge to others in interesting ways. This can be exciting to explore how you'll do that through your words.

While Aquarius is a fixed sign, the moods can be up and down, and they may scatter their energies rather than focus them on something substantial. See if you can find steadiness in the scattered energy. It might take some extra movement and grounding. Since Aquarius is brilliant at reading others, notice what's left unsaid in your verbal and written conversations. This could be fuel for some writing.

Ask good questions and question structures, systems, and old beliefs. You just might have some surprising ideas to change them.

Because Aquarius is the sign of revolution, if you've had a block in your writing project, this could be a powerful time to blast through it with an idea you hadn't had before. Stay open to big breakthroughs. You might also enjoy writing on unconventional topics or in new ways, discovering new connections within your work and to others who can improve your project and take it into the future.

HIGH-VIBE AQUARIUS: Improving something for humanity and the planet and making the world a better place. Taking something existing and tweaking it for the greater good, or reworking and reimagining an old idea entirely into something new. Grounding a big idea into reality.

LOW-VIBE AQUARIUS: Stuck overthinking, being scatter-brained or spacey, or having lack of focus. Negative emotions such as jealousy, possessiveness, and fear could surface. Trying to rise "above" what you consider "pettiness" can sometimes lead to emotional blocks, leaving you feeling detached from your work. Remember your reason for writing in the first place to keep going and find meaning in what you're creating.

Nourishing Body, Mind, Spirit

BODY: Try some calf raises when you take writing breaks and use a ball to massage your feet while you sit at your writing desk. Eat with electronics out of sight because you want to be extra thoughtful of everything you consume—this includes information.

MIND: Instead of resisting a busy mind, let all those seemingly random thoughts out onto the page with pen and paper. Using a pen and paper slows your busy brain down. No judging. Subtle thoughts can disrupt a clear mind. Turn on some upbeat music and let it all out.

SPIRIT: Explore your writing project as an ongoing spiritual journey. What does your soul want to say?

New Moon Actions & Prompts

New Moon Actions

* Make plans for the rest of your writing project with an eye toward the rest of the year.
* Let yourself dream about your vision in as much detail as possible.
* By asking good questions and questioning structures, you might have some fresh and future-focused ideas about how to change them.
* Let your natural genius shine through—no holding back.
* Think about how your writing project affects the collective for the better.
* Commit or recommit to your writing project in this cycle. How can you do it in a way that doesn't just think outside the box but throws away the box?
* Look back at where you were in the weeks leading up to today. Think about where you've grown, how you've changed, and the ways you're different. What do you know now? What do you see now that you didn't see before?
* You might take your intentions from last month and deepen them, tweak them, or even scrap them and start new ones.

New Moon Writing Prompts

What's no longer a part of the story?

I know this to be true . . .

If I could write anything at all, it would be . . .

I'm creating change . . .

I'm committed to . . .

I'm here to . . .

I improve . . .

Cool and calm is needed here . . .

Re-imagining . . .

What I write is unique . . .

Waxing Moon Actions & Prompts

Waxing Moon Actions

* Watch out for your brain trying to bring you into swirling thoughts today. Allow all the writing projects and inspiration to come through and capture all the ideas. Knowing that writing them down doesn't mean you need to take action on them—but taking inspired action is always a good idea, so see if you can get moving on one idea that feels the strongest. Make this decision from your heart, not your head.

* Choose a completely unrelated industry and go exploring—read online or visit the specialty magazine section of a bookstore. You never know what you might find that would relate to your business or writing project.
* Look at any interruptions today as invitations to see things differently and shift your perspective. Offer thanks to every uninvited pause.
* Visit a new place to sit and write today. Make a point to simply observe without judgment what's going on around you.
* Let the writing be what it wants to be. You can decide what to do with it later.
* Indulge in a great brainstorming session. Think about your writing project, even if you invest just fifteen minutes today, having a completely unfiltered brainstorming session without judging your ideas will set you up for later success.
* Allow all the ideas to come through in whatever order they want. You don't need to impose any structure to this; you can simply let it have the boundaries that will come later, or trust that the structure is there under the surface.

Waxing Moon Writing Prompts

What would feel freeing?

This would be cool . . .

What if . . .

I'm curious about . . .

I have so many ideas . . .

This idea is pulling me strongly . . .

I create freely . . .

My writing wants . . .

I offer thanks . . .

I see . . .

Full Moon Actions & Prompts

Full Moon Actions

* Notice something you see now that you didn't before.
* Let your natural genius zone shine through.
* Push boundaries and play with your comfort edges in your writing—whether in the topic, the medium, or a new tech or tool.
* Look at your recent content. Did you ask readers to share? Add a CTA (call to action) to read other articles and sign up for your newsletter.
* Post on social media about an older piece of content that pushed some boundaries.
* Aquarius loves sharing wisdom—share some knowledge confidently in a piece of writing today.
* Ask your readers or followers a thought-provoking question.

* Keep an open mind about information you receive and any words that come out that surprise you.
* Surrender and let go of an idea that's running into a dead end.
* Ideas are great, but only if you take action on them. You don't need to take action on every idea, but it's your responsibility to move some forward. If you've been stockpiling ideas, choose one—trust it's the right one, and take one action today.

Full Moon Writing Prompts

It would be cool to push boundaries here . . .

My readers seem to resonate with . . .

I didn't realize this . . .

I see some trends . . .

What I want my readers to do most . . .

I stand out . . .

I grow personally . . .

I surrender . . .

My genius . . .

I'd love to push boundaries . . .

Waning Moon Actions & Prompts

Waning Moon Actions

* Notice what you're grasping or clinging to that you don't need to reach for your big vision or goals.
* Review your lists of ideas and discern if they came from you or someone else.
* Explore any antiquated structures and systems that no longer serve you and replace them with ones that work for how you create.
* Look back over your writing projects from the past month, and explore where you could have used more support.
* Decide how you'll do things differently in the next moon cycle.
* Edit your work and be mindful of keeping any fear out. Editing out of fear, "What will people think?" or "This needs to be accepted by people," can hinder where you're led to go with your writing. Worrying about what others want can keep you from being inventive right now.

Waning Moon Writing Prompts

I was clinging to this and it's time to let go . . .

I'm experiencing some fear around . . .

I feel the need to be accepted by . . .

If I change this, it'll work better . . .

I'm going to do this differently in the next moon cycle . . .

I'm working to improve . . .

I need some healing here to be able to write what I need to write . . .

I have the freedom to . . .

No more people-pleasing . . .

This serves the world . . .

PISCES

"Anything is possible."

SUN DATES: February 19 - March 20

SYMBOL: The Fish — two fish swimming in opposite directions. In your writing practice, maybe you notice one part of you wants one thing, and another part wants something else.

ELEMENT: Water — the ocean or vapor, dissolving boundaries

MODE: Mutable — endless and changing

ENERGY: Feminine — inward, receptive, intuitive

RULING PLANETS: Jupiter and Neptune

Jupiter (traditional) symbolizes reach, possibility, and broader purpose.

Neptune (modern) is the God of the Sea and considered a planet of inspiration, dreams, psychic receptivity, and illusion.

HOUSE: Twelfth

The Twelfth House represents the subconscious, hidden patterns, and endings. It rules intuition, solitude, dreams, spiritual growth, and the unseen forces that influence your life, as well as the process of release, healing, and surrender.

BODY PARTS: feet, blood, pineal gland, appendix, and lymphatic system, as well as the energetic, emotional, and spiritual body

PAIR: Virgo

METALS: Platinum and Tin

Platinum — represents excitement, calm, and joy, and supports psychic abilities

Tin — represents malleability and flexibility

GEMS:

Amethyst: enhances spirituality

Aquamarine: enhances psychic tendencies

Jade: brings grounding, creativity, balance, and harmony

Lapis Lazuli: supports clear and authentic communication, and tapping into intuition and deeper perception

COLORS:

Lavender: spiritual healing and cosmic consciousness

Sea Green: fertility, renewal, faith

FLOWERS:

Water Lily: spiritual transformation, purity, divine creation, healing, harmony

Violet: intuition and spiritual wisdom

Orchid: grace, elegance, love

ESSENTIAL OILS:

Black Pepper: focus and mental clarity, grounding for boosting concentration and motivation

Sweet Orange: uplifts and energizes a sensitive mind when bogged down with heavy emotions

Cedarwood: helps to bring daydreaming back down to earth

Sandalwood: supports creativity and artistry

Juniper Berry: clears negative energy when overwhelmed by others' emotions

Rose: heart healing, cultivating unconditional love, and restoring a sense of divine feminine wholeness

MANTRAS:

I believe.
My imagination is limitless.
I trust my intuition.

KEYWORDS:

accept, angel, aroma, art, cleanse, closure, compassion, completion, contribution, cure, devote, dreamer, eliminate, empathy, endless, envision, expansive, fantasy, fluid, forgiveness, freedom, healing, imagination, invisible, kindness, love, magical, meal, meditation, music, photography, prayer, preparation, release, romantic, sensitive, serve, spirit, spiritual, sympathy, tender, understanding, unification, unpredictable, unrealistic, water

CONTENT INSPIRATION:

flow • power • what makes us individually unique and still one • journaling • adding emotional layers in big swaths across your writing • empathy and heart-led selling • dreams • intuition • dancing • singing • painting • music • spirituality • creative outlets • the ocean • water • making waves • inspiring people • helping others feel seen, heard, and understood

WRITING WITH THIS SIGN:

As the twelfth and final sign of the zodiac, Pisces represents culmination. After this completion, the zodiac begins again with Aries—the initiating first sign. To be able to begin again, we first need to complete—which is part of preparation.

With the symbol of two fish swimming in different directions, Pisces can sense the reasoning behind multiple dimensions of things. This gives them a full picture of differing opinions and ideas but can sometimes make them seem indecisive or unreliable to others.

Picturing the two fish, one side craves duality, one craves depth. Since Pisces is mutable, changeable, and endless, this might make your writing feel contradictory at times. Let it sit, and revisit it if needed. Or let it be, showing multiple sides to a story.

As a mutable water sign, the water needs to flow freely. Constriction won't feel great. We can hardly contain the ocean: picture how vast the shore is. Rigid writing rules all need to go out the window—you don't need any rules to write. But the lightly structured guidance in this book can give you just the right amount of support you need to let your creativity flow freely.

Pay attention to your dreams, signs, and synchronicities. Notice the language of your intuition. Does your intuition talk to you through feelings, sounds, sights, smells, or knowings? Take the time to notice, feel, and listen.

Listening is an ongoing practice to focus on before, during, and after writing. Our intuition is part of everything we do, especially as intuitive writers—we write with our intuition, not our thinking mind, which tends to force and overwhelm us.

Emotions might feel louder or more potent right now. Instead of letting your emotions drive your decisions, feel them fully for a minute, get curious about them, stay open to the messages behind them, and then move them.

Here's a writing tip I saved for Pisces—since Pisces contains a piece of all the previous signs, you can apply this advice anytime. At the end of your writing session, look at your topic for the next day. Quickly review your notes and then put them away. That's it. Then, first thing in the morning (you know, that state where you're kind of awake but not totally, or even better if you can wake up naturally), bring your topic to mind and let your mind wander. It's not about forcing or making it happen but rather letting your unconscious mind do the work.

This way, when you arrive at the page, your mind has already been rolling the idea around. This is another sneaky way to move past writing resistance; when you let the ideas reverberate in your brain for a while, you might find more excitement to get to the page. You could even be itching to let all the words out.

Another way to approach this little brain game is to write about one topic a week. Say it's for blog content or a book chapter. On the weekend, review your notes and think about what you want to say without trying to get any of the words down. Over time, you're training your unconscious mind to do the heavy lifting for you. So when you come to the blank page to write, you might find the words are there waiting, ready to flow out.

HIGH-VIBE PISCES: Trusting your connection with God and the messages you get for your higher self. Embracing kindness, intuition, and sweetness. Allowing your fully creative, multi-faceted self to show through in all your writing projects.

LOW-VIBE PISCES: Letting yourself get lost in your own mind, being careless with addictions, or looking for an escape—whether through substances like drugs or alcohol or scrolling, sex, shopping, or overworking. Low-vibe Pisces can be ungrounded and can't seem to make progress on anything. Earthly things like bills, false time constructs, and the like can feel heavy. Look to balance the ungroundedness with practicality, remembering how even a body of water as vast as the ocean has a container.

Nourishing Body, Mind, Spirit

BODY: Sip a ceremonial raw cacao latte as you write. Cacao supports the pineal gland and your intuition. Feel your feet firmly planted on the ground throughout the day. Stretch your toes, maybe rolling them over a ball—especially if you've got a lot of sitting and writing planned.

MIND: Let go of the restrictions and limitations of your thinking mind and suspend old ways of thinking so you can begin with renewed energy when the moon moves into Aries. Let yourself immerse your thoughts and imagination into the world you want to see.

SPIRIT: Look after your spirit and soul as well as you look after your body.

New Moon Actions & Prompts

New Moon Actions

* Be as gentle with yourself today as you are with everyone else.
* Go with the flow within a large container of time by putting a few hours on your calendar with the permission to really explore your creativity.
* Notice the subtle messages in your journal pages. Write slowly so you can spot them.
* If you feel pulled in different directions, use this time to meditate on any unmade writing decisions and even consider writing in one direction before exploring another.
* Choose your next writing project based on what your soul wants to write—it might surprise you. Or rather, let your writing project find you.
* As you write new moon intentions, see yourself as the best version of you.
* Use an online thesaurus to expand your emotional vocabulary and explore how you, your readers, or clients want to feel.
* Stay open to Divine guidance by staying relaxed as you write. We can't hear God when we're stressed.
* Visualize your new self as you write new moon intentions—what are you wearing? What perfume are you spritzing on?

New Moon Writing Prompts

This will feel like medicine today . . .

My reader wants to feel . . .

My deepest desire . . .

My soul craves . . .

I listen . . .

Life is happening for me . . .

I savor the sweetness . . .

The words flow out of my fingertips effortlessly . . .

I trust my flow . . .

I bring compassion . . .

Waxing Moon Actions & Prompts

Waxing Moon Actions

* As you write today, imagine your words are a fountain and you have the power to turn the faucet open or closed. When you sit down to write, let the words that have been building up pour out. No judgment, forcing, or editing as you write your draft.
* If you feel foggy before writing, spend some time with your journal pages first, perhaps while sitting in the sun. Even five minutes following one of the writing prompts in this book will help you find clarity.

- If you're writing sales-focused copy or content, put yourself in your readers' shoes today—see what they see, feel what they feel, hear what they hear, and write to that.
- Take a bath to calm a busy mind. Consider adding some essential oils listed earlier.
- Create healthy ways to pause when you're craving an escape —be in or around water, take a bath, stay hydrated, drink from blue glass bottles. I like to keep these bottles filled with filtered water and let them sit in the sun for a few hours before drinking.

Waxing Moon Writing Prompts

I'm feeling these emotions right now . . .

This is bubbling over and spilling onto the page . . .

I connect . . .

I think I want __ but what I really need is . . .

This dream has been popping up lately . . .

I write with empathy . . .

I bring calm . . .

My favorite way to recenter myself . . .

My well of writing inspiration . . .

This drama is not mine . . .

Full Moon Actions & Prompts

Full Moon Actions

* Stay present, no matter how uncomfortable it is at first, instead of trying to escape or check out.
* Notice where you're comparing your current self to your past self. You've changed, the moon has changed signs, your hormones have changed—give yourself grace.
* Stay open to how your writing project wants to move or change directions. Like the ocean, it's wild, unpredictable, and splashes up onto the shore. Flow with it instead of fighting it.
* Make time for a journaling session to write as much as you want on all the themes flowing through your mind right now.
* Release things that aren't serving your best writing life, like carelessness and unhealthy lifestyle choices.
* Notice where you may be staying stuck out of worry or fear and let these grips go.

Full Moon Writing Prompts

My inner writer needs healing . . .

I'm letting go of this dream . . .

I'm making space for . . .

These emotions feel strong right now . . .

I refocus . . .

I no longer fight . . .

Unpredictability . . .

My soul . . .

Healing is . . .

Flexibility brings . . .

Waning Moon Actions & Prompts

Waning Moon Actions

* Do an emotional edit to your writing, sprinkling in feeling words where needed.
* Go into your work in progress or revisit an old piece of writing and intuitively see where your words need more feeling.
* Carve out some time to take a breath and be near water or in water to be fully present.
* As you edit, be mindful of any self-criticism and fault-finding.
* Allow yourself to get lost in a large editing project with the freedom to flow to different sections or pages.

Waning Moon Writing Prompts

I feel most in flow when . . .

I'm going to let this float away before the next new moon . . .

I hear . . .

My writing really needs this from me . . .

Flowing . . .

When still and quiet, I feel . . .

Feelings are . . .

I find power in flowing with . . .

I bring grace . . .

I am awake . . .

WHAT'S NEXT

By now, you know that you don't get to a feel-good writing practice by thinking. You get there by feeling your way there and taking action. My advice is to keep going through the prompts and advice in these pages. You can use this book as your trusted writing companion to flow with you every day for at least the next year. Every day, you can work with a new prompt, and with a different keyword or theme as the days flow through each sign. Writing and editing over and over is how you build a beautiful, nourishing writing practice.

Listening is also an ongoing practice to focus on before, during, and after writing. Our intuition is part of everything we do, especially as intuitive writers—we write with our intuition, not our thinking mind, which tends to doubt, force, and overwhelm us.

If you're having fun and seeing the evidence in your life and writing by working with the daily moon, consider planning your writing, business, and of course your life by using the astrology of the day. Begin by looking at your calendar for the coming week. Find out what sign the moon will be in on those days. You might realize that your schedule lines up perfectly—it often does. For example, you might discover that your day filled with back-to-back meetings can feel extra draining during a Pisces moon but exciting during a Libra moon.

As you get to know how it feels to flow with the energy of the zodiac signs, you can schedule particular writing tasks to happen on certain days. Perhaps you'll draft your blog posts during a Gemini moon, edit your website with some emotional words during the Cancer moon, and refine your author bio when the moon's in Virgo.

However you decide to work with the daily moon, remember to keep it light, fun, and to use it as a suggestion, not a prescription to tap into your unique flow.

JOIN THE INTUITIVE WRITING STUDIO

You've already started. Now keep going—with support.

The Intuitive Writing Studio is where writers and author-entrepreneurs come to write with the moon every day. This book is the framework — the Studio is where you step into daily practice.

Co-writing sessions, daily prompts, monthly workshops, coaching, and a community of people who get it.

No burnout. No forcing. Just a writing practice that finally feels good.

As a reader, mention the book when you join—and you'll get a free 30-minute coaching call to get moving on your specific writing challenge.

Join us at theintuitivewritingschool.com/community

GRATITUDE

To my online writing community and clients—you stepped into this daily experiment with me, returning to the page again and again for over two years as I tested and refined these practices and prompts. Thank you for your curiosity, your courage, and your willingness to surrender to the process.

To my editors and proofreaders, thank you for helping my voice come through clearly and cleanly on every page.

For my God-given voice, medicine, gifts, and talents—may I continue to honor and use them fully.

And, of course, to my husband and our two children, thank you for loving and supporting me through it all—and for humoring me when I inevitably say, "Guys, come look at the moon!"

RESOURCES

Before you procrasti-learn (delay the inevitable writing you know you need to do by researching astrology), hold on. The best way to find your writing flow is to write. You just read enough. You are enough. Now, it's time to take action—if you haven't already.

If you want to explore a few more books and tools on the topics of astrology and writing, find a current list of recommendations here:

www.theintuitivewritingschool.com/wwtm-resources

ABOUT THE AUTHOR

JACQUELINE FISCH believes your best writing happens when you stop forcing it. As an author, writing coach, and founder of The Intuitive Writing School, she helps authors and entrepreneurs move through perfectionism, self-doubt, and writer's block to finish the book or start the blog they've been dreaming about for years.

With over twenty years as a communications professional, Jacqueline now dedicates herself fully to helping writers and entrepreneurs tell their stories authentically, stand out, and make an impact.

Her approach blends practical strategy with intuitive, energy-led practices, guiding writers to tap into their own creative rhythm—and yes, sometimes the moon.

Jacqueline is a Libra Sun, Pisces Moon, Aries Rising.

www.jacquelinefisch.com

www.ingramcontent.com/pod-product-compliance
Lightning Source LLC
LaVergne TN
LVHW091205150826
845672LV00005B/1251

* 9 7 8 1 7 3 6 5 5 4 2 6 5 *